Shirley Hegarty 1985
From
Cathy + George
4/24

D0712784

THE
INNER STORY

*Myth and Symbol
in the Bible
and Literature*

HELEN M. LUKE

CROSSROAD · NEW YORK

1982
The Crossroad Publishing Company
575 Lexington Avenue, New York, NY 10022

Printed in the United States of America

Library of Congress Cataloging in Publication Data

Luke, Helen M., 1904–
    The inner story

    1. Myth in literature—Addresses, essays, lectures.
    2. Symbolism in literature—Addresses, essays, lectures.
    3. Myth in the Bible—Addresses, essays, lectures.
    4. Symbolism in the Bible—Addresses, essays, lectures.
    I. Title.
    PN56.M94L84   809'.15   81-17473
    ISBN 0-8245-0443-7   AACR2

ACKNOWLEDGMENTS

Euripides, *The Bacchae*, translated by William Arrowsmith,
from *The Complete Greek Tragedies*, ed. David Grene and
Richmond Lattimore. Copyright © 1959 by The University
of Chicago. All rights reserved. Published 1959.
First Phoenix edition, 1968.

Contents

Foreword *vii*

Introduction 1

An African Tale 5

The Story of the Exodus 12

The Bacchae, by Euripides 36

The Little Prince, by Antoine de Saint-Exupéry 54

The Story of Saul 65

Frodo's Mithril Coat in *The Lord of the Rings,* 74
by J. R. R. Tolkien

"The King and the Corpse" 80

The Symbolism of Water in the Bible 90

The Story of Jacob 98

King Lear, by Shakespeare 113

Foreword

Yeats once wrote, "There is but the one history and that the soul's."* That there is such a history—a story we need to know, *the* story of the soul—is a fact that has been known to healers since the Stone Age, but it is not a commonplace any longer. Everything Helen Luke has written says that there is such a history and here, by way of commentary on ten ancient and more recent tales, she reveals this inner story in a way which again gently but urgently invites one to undertake the living of it—to enter upon the way.

At the beginning of her essay on Moses, she writes, "Now we turn to the story of a man who hears the inner voice and who is willing to pay, step by step, the great price that is asked of one who will be obedient to it." Isaiah, Paul, or Black Elk would recognize this language immediately, the language of inner voice and guiding image, of surrender and conscious obedience to a power and presence other than one's self. The language of such demand has become unwelcome and unfamiliar to us, the histories it relates impenetrable, to our immeasurable loss. Helen Luke is a guide to the relearning of such language and the reading of its stories, both in her writing and in her work as a therapist.

---

* The quotation from Yeats is from the introduction to the 1928 version of *A Vision*.

I remember the excitement with which, some years ago, I first read Mrs. Luke's essays on Saul, Jacob, and Moses and shared them with students. At the time, they helped us, a group of colleagues, to shape a humanities seminar at Notre Dame, a series of readings and discussions to assist us to discover "the one history." On many occasions since then, I have given copies of these and other of Mrs. Luke's essays to individuals who stood in urgent need of discovering the inner story in themselves, when only the discovery of this fact could keep them from losing their way, from suffering what the old healers called "loss of soul."

Usually brief and always unpretentious, the essays in this book speak with the authority of one who has herself long been living the inner story consciously and with grace. As she has become older, Mrs. Luke's wisdom has become ever more direct—simpler and more obedient to the inner voice, the guiding image. It is a rare privilege to meet such a person, especially in our time, and we are indebted to the publisher for again persuading her to allow some of her essays to be published.

John C. Gerber, C.S.C.
University of Notre Dame

Introduction

The essence of all religions, from the most primitive to the most highly developed, has always been expressed by the human soul in stories. The Mass itself is a story—a symbolic drama telling the great story of the death and resurrection of Christ. We can say, "I believe in this or that," and assert the truth of many doctrines, but these things will not affect the soul of any one of us unless in some way we experience their meaning through intense response to the images conveyed in story. Innumerable tales in all ages have expressed the changing relationships of human beings to their gods and have told of their search for the divine meaning behind their lives.

Before the invention of writing all human knowledge was conveyed from generation to generation by storytellers who were the sacred minstrels and medicine men of the people; and, even after the growth of consciousness had brought about the formulation of doctrines and the definitions of dogma, the great storytellers kept alive into our own day the imaginative response to the numinous, which alone gives life to conceptual dogma.

In the first chapter of this book there is a quotation from Harold Goddard, who said of the history of the world, "The destiny of the world is determined less by the battles that are lost and won than by the stories it loves and believes in" (*The Meaning of Shakespeare*, Vol. 2, p. 208). We may see a light of hope in the darkness of our lives when we hear that so many theologians and psychologists nowadays are joining the poets in affirming anew the tremendous importance of story. A friend who is a theologian was saying to me the other day that, valuable as conceptual theory is, it can only speak to the intellectual faculties in men and women; whereas in a story the living confrontation of the opposites and the transcendent symbol that resolves conflict speak directly to the listener's mind, heart and imagination in the same images.

C. G. Jung has told us how he found, after his own lonely confrontation with the powers of the unconscious, the life-giving wonder of the inner myth, or story, behind his life; and it is in part by our response to the great stories of the world that we too can begin to find, each of us, this individual story, expressing the symbolic meaning behind the facts of our fate and behind the motives that determine the day-to-day choices of our lives. If we are not aware of the need for this imaginative search, and continue to base our attitudes purely on the kind of thinking that is bounded by the laws of materialistic cause and effect and statistical data, then sooner or later we shall be forced to see how the springs of life dry up, and how nature, physical as well as psychic, is gradually polluted and sterilized, so that we look forward to a time when there will be no pure water left for us to drink. Yet there is a steadily growing hope in the increasing number of people who drink from the life-giving springs of the images within, and this book is simply a collection of studies made with small groups over the years, as we looked at some of the great stories, ancient and modern, and sought to realize their meaning in our lives.

The experience of darkness, of evil, is essential to redemption and there is no inner story that does not contain this truth. As Judas and the Pharisees were essential to Christ's death and resurrection, so in every story of the soul, the tiny flame of love and awareness is threatened with extinction, and saved only through the humility and sacrifice of an individual human being.

At the end of his life, C. G. Jung (as we can see in his later letters) continually stressed that *only* if enough individuals would commit themselves totally to this search, each for his or her own inner truth, could the world avoid disaster. The inner story, though the same in essence for all, is always single and unique in each human being, never before lived and never to be repeated.

The Inner Story

An African Tale [*]

real story touches not only the mind, but also the imagination and the unconscious depths in a person, and it may remain with him or her through many years, coming to the surface of consciousness now and then to yield new insights. A great teacher of English at Swarthmore College, the late Harold Goddard, wrote in his book *The Meaning of Shakespeare,* "The destiny of the world is determined less by the battles that are lost and won than by the stories it loves and believes in."[1] I heard the following story a number of years ago told by Laurens van der Post at a conference.[2] He had heard it from a Zulu wise man in Africa, and he was retelling it as an offering of gratitude and respect to the women of the world.

All those stories that deal with basic human themes draw their power from the archetypal world that is common to people of all cultures and of all times, but the images in each culture will, of course, differ greatly, and it is for us to penetrate through

---

* This chapter was previously published in the Summer 1981 *Courier,* the alumnae quarterly of St. Mary's College, Notre Dame, Indiana. It formed a part of Helen Luke's commencement address to the St. Mary's College Class of 1981.
[1] Harold Goddard, *The Meaning of Shakespeare,* vol. 2 (Chicago: University of Chicago Press, 1965), p. 208.
[2] Story told by Laurens van der Post at the Notre Dame Jung Conference, Notre Dame, Indiana, 1973. He has warmly approved Helen Luke's use of it.

these varying pictures to the universal wisdom that underlies them. I propose to tell the story first, simply, as it is told in its African context; and afterwards I will go through it again with a few indications as to how it may yield its wisdom in terms of our own lives. It is a story about young women on the threshold of their adult lives—and that is a rare thing to find. There is no hero in it at all—only one somewhat devastating male figure!

In an African village a group of young women had banded together to humiliate one of their number of whom they were jealous and whom they had rejected because she was "different," and especially because it seemed to them that she had a necklace of beads that was more beautiful than their necklaces.

These jealous young women ran down to the banks of the river and there they planned a trap for the envied one. When she joined them, they told her that they had all thrown their necklaces into the river as an offering to the river god. The young woman was a person of generous heart, so she at once took off her own necklace and threw it into the river; whereupon the others dug up their necklaces, which they had buried in the sand, and went off laughing and sneering.

The young woman, left alone, was very sad. She had been duped into a well-meant but foolish act, and she wandered along the riverbank, praying to the god to restore the necklace. There was no answer until at last she heard a voice, bidding her plunge into a deep pool nearby. She did not hesitate, for she knew it was the voice of the god. She plunged down into the unknown and found herself on the riverbed, where an old woman sat waiting. This old one was exceedingly ugly, even repulsive, for she was covered with open sores, and she spoke to the girl, saying, "Lick my sores!" At once the girl obeyed out of her compassionate heart, and licked the repulsive sores as she had been asked to do. Then the old woman said to her, "Because you have not held back and have licked my sores, I will hide and protect you when the demon comes who devours the flesh of young women." At that she heard a roar and a huge male monster came, calling out that he smelled a maiden there. But the old woman had hidden her away, and soon he went off cursing.

Then the old woman said to the girl, "Here is your necklace"—and she put around her neck beads of far greater beauty than any she had had before. "Go back now," the old woman said, "to your village, but when you have gone a few yards from the pool, you will see a stone in the path. Pick up this rock and throw it back into the pool. Then go on without looking back and take up your ordinary life in your village."

The young woman obeyed. She found the stone and threw it back and came to the village without a backward look. There the other girls quickly noticed her beautiful new necklace and clamored to know where she had found it—to which she replied that it had been given to her by the old woman at the bottom of the pool in the river. Not waiting for more, they all rushed off in a body and jumped into the pool. And the old woman said to each of them as she had said before, "Lick my sores!" But these girls all laughed at her and said they wouldn't dream of doing anything so repulsive—and useless, too—and they demanded to be given necklaces at once. In the midst of all this there came the roar of the giant demon, who seized upon those girls, one after the other, and made a mighty meal of them. And with that the story comes to an end.

I shall now look briefly at the images in the story as symbols of certain attitudes, conscious or unconscious, that are alive in each one of us and influence us in often unrealized and subtle ways. Stories like this are not manufactured by the intellect; they are the symbolic dreams of humanity.

The necklace in Africa is a highly prized symbol of a woman's identity and worth as a person. The group of girls in the story play a particularly unkind trick since it concerns devotion to a divine, transpersonal value. It is the product of group mentality, mass thinking, which so often covers and excuses hatred and cruelty. This is perhaps the worst menace in our society, requiring great effort and integrity to resist.

Notice the ease with which the simple girl falls into the trap. This is surely a warning of the dangers that lie in wait for the generous-hearted, who are so quickly induced by the slogans of some cause or crusade, fine in itself perhaps, and sponsored by

people we long to please. We lose sight of our individual responsibility to reflect and to *choose,* and thus, as it were, we throw
away our identity. Nevertheless, the story goes on to show us
that such naive enthusiasms, *if* they truly involve the intention
of a personal sacrifice to that which is greater than our egos, to
the river of life itself, may indeed bring about the shock that
leads us out of group thinking to the discovery of our meaning as
individuals on a much deeper level.

The young woman in the story had a rude awakening from her
identification with her peers. We may notice that she did not
waste energy on resentment or remorse. She stayed alone beside
the river of life, praying that she might rediscover her value as a
person, waiting for an inner voice to bring her wisdom. And it
came. She was to look for her necklace down under the water.
Only by going *down,* not by striving upwards, would she find
herself. She must plunge into the river of life *unconditionally,*
risking mistakes or failure, not just throwing things, however
valuable, into the river. Only by trusting herself to the unknown,
both in her outer life and in her own hidden depths, would she
find her unique way.

This young woman was now obedient, not to convention or
opinions or slogans, but to that voice from within that may be
heard by us all at the crucial moments of life, if we will truly
listen.

She plunged down into the pool and there she found—not a
radiant woman, symbolizing her potential beauty and power,
but an old, ugly, repulsive thing with open sores. How shall we
read this image for ourselves? When we enter with open eyes
into the river of live, we find ourselves face to face with the ug-
liness, the suffering from which we have perhaps been protected
hitherto in many different ways. And it is now that the story
yields to us its specifically *feminine* wisdom.

We may take this image of the old woman on two levels. She
may stand for the suffering that contempt for the feminine
values has brought to all women through the ages—a contempt
of which not only many men have been guilty, but also large

numbers of women themselves, especially in our time. And secondly, the old woman is an image on the personal level of the most despised and repellent things in our own psyches that we refuse to acknowledge and from which we turn often in disgust.

The old woman's invitation is clear. "You can't bring help to me by any kind of technical, scientific, impersonal and collective panacea, or by *talk about* justice and freedom. Only with your own saliva can you bring healing to these sores in yourself and in the world." Saliva is symbolically a healing water that we are all born with. The licking of an animal is its one means of healing wounds, and we may remember Christ's saliva on the blind man's eyes. So the girl is asked to give of her own unique essence—to bring healing to the sores, not by words out of her mouth but by water from her mouth. Because she is on the threshold of true womanhood the girl at once responds out of that essential core of the feminine being—the compassionate heart. Here I would emphasize that true compassion bears *no* resemblance to a vague and sentimental pity. Compassion is not just an emotion; it is an austere thing and a highly differentiated quality of soul.

And now comes that universal threat—the demon of inferior masculinity that can so easily devour our womanhood. When this happens, we simply lose ourselves in an imitation of men, which kills the truly creative masculine spirit in a woman, and, however outwardly successful she may be, all hope of equality of *value* in the world of men disappears.

Had there been a male "hero" present, we might imagine the old woman telling him to take up his sword and fight the monster of greed and aggression. But to every woman she will always say, "Because of your compassion you will be freed from him."

So it came about that the devouring ambition and greed had no power over the woman who had the courage and humility to lick the repellent sores. It is at this moment that she receives her own individual and unique necklace—she does not just recover the old one that had come from her family before her initiation into life. This necklace is hers and hers alone.

It is time to return to her life in the world, to the daily, ordinary tasks and relationships. In her case, marriage and children awaited her and the building of a home; in our time and place, a career most probably awaits her, with or without the ancient way of woman in the home. But whether she marries and bears children or not, this ancient responsibility of woman remains. She is the guardian of the values of feeling in her environment, and if she remains aware of that compassion, that quiet, hidden nurturing that is the center of her feminine nature, then her skills in any kind of work whatsoever will grow in the manner of trees, well rooted and strong, and her creative spirit will be free. The woman who has received the necklace from the old woman in the pool does not seek compulsively to achieve success after success, collecting necklace after necklace, so to speak. Always she will remember to "lick the sores" and to remain still and hidden when the demon of greedy ambition threatens, whether at home or in the public arena.

Now as to the stone that the girl was to find and throw back, I'll give you one hint and leave you to work it out. The stone in all cultures is the symbol of the immortal self, and this is the true offering to the divinity in the river. Don't pick it up and put it in your pocket!

The last bit of the story speaks for itself. All those greedy girls who did not bother to reflect on the meaning of life went rushing off in a mob, all wanting more and better necklaces, which in our day would be more and more demands for wealth, or success, or men, or publicity, or security, or even for spiritual experiences. They refused with contempt the essential task of a woman, the compassionate "licking of the sores" in themselves and in their immediate environment. They were therefore devoured by the demon that rages around, assimilating such women to itself.

Charles Williams, the English poet and novelist who died in 1946, once defined the art of living as the ability "to live the ordinary in an extraordinary way and to live the extraordinary in an ordinary way." The story illuminates this beautiful saying.

Dame Janet Baker, a great singer and a great woman, said recently in an interview, "I've found that the ordinary things are the important things. . . . We all—in life and music—have our backs up against the wall trying to preserve order and quality. . . . My gift is God-given and it must be given back. We all have a gift to give, and if you give it with a sense of holy obligation everything clicks into place."

Each of us, as we journey through life, has the opportunity to find and to give his or her unique gift. Whether that gift is great or small in the eyes of the world does not matter at all—not at all; it is through the finding and the giving that we may come to know the joy that lies at the center of both the dark times and the light.

The Story of the Exodus

I t is possible to read the story of the exodus from Egypt as the inner life history of three kinds of people. Moses is the hero, the man of great capabilities, of imagination and vision, born to be a leader, whose integrity of will remains unshaken by success or adversity. Pharaoh is equally a man born to lead, but his will is corrupted by power and luxury so that he is incapable, in the end, even in the face of conclusive evidence, of recognizing the truth of any fact that threatens his pride or his comfort. The children of Israel in their slavery to Pharaoh, in their response to Moses, in their long endurance in the wilderness, in their alternating faith and grumbling disobedience, in their courage and their cowardice, are ordinary people; they stumble along with many falls and backslidings, but they retain the fundamental good will that keeps them journeying in spite of everything toward the promised land. Each individual enduring in the wilderness carries within himself or herself the Moses image and the Pharaoh image—the hero and the renegade—and only at the journey's end will the struggle between these be resolved.

Pharaoh

There are actually two Pharaohs in the story; the son succeeded the father during Moses' exile, but for our purpose we may take them as one symbolic figure. Pharaoh was born to the purple, to riches and power, but one does not have to be a king to have such an inheritance. One may be born with other kinds of inherited wealth—money, social position, riches of intellect, artistic ability, or bodily strength, all of which mean that one is in a position to exercise power without having done much to earn it. One may do this harmlessly for a while, as did Pharaoh, but the test will surely come that will either shock a person into the beginnings of detachment from this power or will plunge him or her into a course of ever-increasing identification with it.

Pharaoh's test is clearly stated. He suddenly became aware that the people of Israel, who had been his predecessor's friends and respected allies, were rapidly increasing in numbers and were becoming rich and prosperous, and he felt himself threatened because he was both jealous and afraid. Jealousy and fear—these are the insidious enemies that in all of us may start a landslide; but they are also Lucifer in his role as light-bringer. A violent, negative emotion of some kind is about the only thing which has power enough to jerk us out of complacency and give us the chance to recognize that we are evading our own shadow side. Pharaoh had a choice thrust upon him. He could have looked at his jealousy and fear and recognized them as signs of unconscious weakness and insecurity hiding under his conscious sense of power and security. Then the strength of the Israelites would have been spent in Egypt's service, and his personality would have acquired depth and wisdom. Instead he gave rein to his fears, decided to enslave and *use* for personal ends this increasing power in the land, this potentiality in his soul. In order to protect himself, he chose to maintain his conscious, one-sided view "lest they multiply; and it comes to pass that, when there falleth any war, they join unto our enemies and fight against us" (Exod. 1:10).

How right he is! If we do not recognize the seemingly alien thing in the unconscious, it will certainly fight against us—against our assumptions of power and invulnerability. We very often do as Pharaoh did—repress the growing power of this alien thing, appoint "overseers" to keep it within bounds, and thus we steal the energy (which would be freely available to us in creative form if we would allow these repressed instincts to speak *their* truth) and make it work for us to increase our sense of importance and power. "And they built for Pharaoh treasure cities" (Exod. 1:11). We need not look far for examples of this. A man obsessed with making money has almost always phenomenal amounts of energy and capacity for work. He will swallow up competitor after competitor with growing ruthlessness and skill, not because he needs more money, but because to stop driving ahead would mean that the enslaved Israelites within him, whose energy he steals, would immediately revolt; his image of himself would be threatened. So also with any drive for power, no matter how dressed up as good work, which becomes for a man or woman a *necessity*. A woman who must dominate through emotional ties or through compulsive work for others, a scholar who must defeat his colleagues in argument, an actor who must hold the center of the stage at the expense of the play and of his colleagues, an unsuccessful person who must always be a victim, often displaying real ruthlessness in establishing this—all are enslaving the strong, free energy of the alien in the soul that threatens the dominance of the ego's demands.

The pressure from below does not, however, decrease. On the contrary, it increases. The Israelites continue to multiply and Pharaoh resorts to new stratagems. He tries to persuade the midwives of the Israelites cruelly to destroy the male children as they are born, but the midwives "feared God" and would not obey. This perhaps may be seen as the first indication in the story that on his feminine feeling side, Pharaoh has some repressed strength and integrity, and we may find in this the reason why he is given so many chances for awakening. There is no record of his ever having shown cruelty toward women. Now he makes no attempt to coerce or punish the midwives. His true, though deeply buried, feeling, symbolized by the midwives, will not commit the murder of the children. The conscious Pharaoh, however, will not listen to this and sends his own *men* to kill the male children, though he does charge them to save the girls—an interesting point, since most ancient civilizations tended to care little for the death of a female child.

The next incident makes this saving grace in Pharaoh even more clear. His daughter (her personal feeling side) actually saves and adopts the Israelite baby who is to become his greatest enemy but who is potentially his savior, the one who will offer him chance after chance for redemption. Pharaoh's feelings are still working for him, raising up in his own family, in his personal unconscious, a strong saving shadow figure whom Pharaoh will eventually be forced to confront in full consciousness. It is a case of the shadow carrying the positive values, as is always the case when a man lives out the dark side of his personality. Through the years, the rejected shadow, whether positive or negative, grows always stronger until it is finally accepted or rejected with the ultimate "yes" or "no."

Pharaoh becomes aware of Moses as a force to be reckoned with when the latter, grown to manhood, is aroused by pity for his people and kills one of the overseers. The boy he has allowed to grow up in his house, who has served him well as soldier, and whom he never thought to fear, suddenly becomes a threat. Moses is driven out into exile for many years. It is as though Pharaoh represses violently a twinge of conscience, and so again his evil will gains added strength. But the repressed shadow in his banishment is also gathering strength, making contact with the deeply buried divine nature, with God himself, whom the conscious Pharaoh denies. When the time is ripe, the shadow, filled now with numinous power, returns, and Pharaoh can no longer evade the confrontation with himself.

Pharaoh is first asked by Moses with respect and courtesy to grant the Hebrews three days' freedom in the wilderness so that they may offer sacrifice there to God. So we may be asked to give up in some very small matter the thing upon which we base our security—a woman to let her child be free to make a mistake; a rich man to risk giving money where will get no return, not even a sense of virtue; an actor to refuse the limelight so that another may be recognized; an analyst to refuse patients when he is already too busy to give any time to his wife and to his inner life. A small and temporary thing, it seems, and yet, of course, we sense, as did Pharaoh, that to give way in this matter would mean to set foot on the way to total loss of the sense of importance and power we have built by enslaving our inner Hebrews. We cannot let them worship the true God, or we might be forced to recognize his validity ourselves, to change the whole direction of our lives. We protest that we have no use for the new value offered to us, but nevertheless there is an uneasy doubt in us, a fear that perhaps this new thing comes from a power greater than ourselves and our gods of possessiveness—and we look for "signs." We are given them in full measure.

In the exodus story the rod becomes a serpent when Aaron throws it down, and it turns back into a rod when he picks it up. Could that perhaps mean for Pharaoh that he is shown in an image that to let go of the rod of his authority means to let loose a serpent, indeed, to free a threatening unconscious content, but that if he faces it, seizes it again, he will not lose his true authority? That is easy, he replies, my magicians can do that. In other words, I can do this kind of thing on *my* terms, make sure the generous gesture doesn't really cost my anything, and pick up the rod quickly on the same old terms, changing nothing.

Pharaoh dismisses Moses and Aaron with mockery and increases his cruelty to the Hebrews. The first chance is refused and his evil will grows stronger. But the repressed content also grows stronger and is filled with ever more numinous power. When the inner voice has been refused and rejected, the series of plagues begins. The river turns to blood, frogs invade the land, then gnats, then flies, followed by disease, boils, hail, locusts, blinding sandstorms. Having refused the opportunity of free choice, Pharaoh is now given chance after chance through *fear* to come to his awakening, to arrest his descent into hell. Most of us have experienced this. Very few make the vital turn without a severe jolt—terrifying dreams, a loss, an accident, an illness, a disabling neurosis—"the gifts of God," as Jung says. We are shocked into awareness as was Pharaoh. But often, too, we follow Pharaoh's pattern of going back on our recognition of the truth. After each plague was removed, he forgot his fear and began to rationalize. We say, "It was only a dream," or "These things were simply bad luck without any meaning. It won't happen again. I can go on as before. The stock market has recovered; I can ease my loss with distractions; I can take care not to have another accident; my neurotic symptoms can be cured with pills." And so on.

The plagues we may compare with warnings coming from different layers of the unconscious. The first is the turning of the water of the river into blood. When there is a moment of choice, such as Moses offered Pharaoh by courteously asking for the release of the Israelites, and the new way is refused, then the unconscious turns hostile. We dream of running in panic from some threat or murderer, an animal, an earthquake, an invasion, and so on. The waters of the Nile no longer nourish the fields of Egypt but spread corruption and breed the next plague of loathsome frogs that invade the land.

So the waters of the unconscious, when rejected, will cease to fertilize our lives and will breed images and other happenings to plague us. Nevertheless, it is clear in this story, as in all human life, that there is purpose behind all this. The plagues, we may say, begin with things that Pharaoh in his palace could no doubt keep at a distance, but the pressure grows greater after each refusal, as though the devil is forcing the individual to the extremity in which he or she may find redemption.

The frogs are the first thing to emerge from the corrupted water, and in all legends and fairy stories they are the symbol of that which appears ugly and loathsome to a human being, but if accepted, or eaten and digested, will work a great transformation. The frog bride or bridegroom can become princess or prince only if wholly accepted in the hideous form of the toad. Nietzsche refused to swallow the repellent creature in his vision, though he knew that he should do so, and it was this refusal that turned him finally onto the way that led to his madness. He was henceforth committed to his identification with the superman. So also Pharaoh.

After the frogs come flying insects, gnats, and then flies—the symbol of the fragmentation of the unconscious. In a fragmented state the mind and the emotions have no center, no root in reality and love. Every little thing is an irritation; our nerves go to pieces. We are frantic and promise ourselves that we will work now on our basic attitudes, that we will face these things, set free the imprisoned energy. For a week, perhaps, we work on our dreams; the gnats and flies decrease; we are relieved. But the effort to focus our attention each day soon ceases. The interval of peace is short and this time the rejected value strikes deeper. The next plagues are diseases and boils. The body is affected and Pharaoh can no longer retreat into his palace. We may know the physical symptoms are psychosomatic, and again we are afraid and promise, as Pharaoh did, to say "yes" to the inner demand, only to fall back as soon as we have the comforting thought that it was "nothing but" a temporary physical illness. Locusts follow, devouring every growing thing, every blade of grass, leaving behind a complete aridity of soul. Again we promise; again we deny. Even the terror of the blinding sandstorm choking all vision, blotting out the sun, hiding man from man, crippling all activity, does not succeed for more than a little while. The wind of the spirit blowing over the aridity of the psyche brings complete blindness and isolation from humanity, instead of the freshness of inspiration and the spark of vision and creative work.

One last disaster is left whereby Pharaoh may be shaken out of his blindness. All the plagues so far can be rationalized away as temporary bad luck. Not so the loss of the greatest value, the most precious thing, his first-born son, his heir, the one he seems to have loved most genuinely. Almost all of us have to come to this last-ditch situation in one form or another, and if we do not embrace it willingly and consciously, sacrificing, letting go of our first-born, our greatest value, our seemingly best, most cherished accomplishment, then, by the grace of God, the experience will come to us outwardly in the form of loss or failure.

The last-ditch situation is constantly appearing in the vital dreams of our lives, and in all legend, all real storytelling, it is this kind of situation that carries the power and meaning of the tale.

The death of the son is Pharaoh's last and supreme chance of redemption. He does not take it. He collapses, gives in, cannot get rid of the Israelites quickly enough, and for a moment, it seems that he will really face himself and the suffering of a change of heart.

At this point Pharaoh could have accepted the death of his son and his own responsibility for it and allowed true repentance to enter his heart. Then death would have become a sacrifice and the transformation of his will would have begun. But he could not face it. His disintegration, checked for a moment, took hold again, fed this time by bitter, blinding hatred. He pursued the children of Israel with all his chariots and horsemen and men of war, thinking to trap them between sea and mountain. But the sea of the unconscious opened before Moses, as it opens for all who will set forth on the inner journey with integrity, and it closed over the strength of Pharaoh, just as it swallows all those who make what Dante called "the great refusal."

Moses

Now we turn to the story of the life of the man who hears the inner voice and who is willing to pay, step by step, the great price which is asked of one who will be obedient to it.

The story of Moses' birth under the threat of murder by Pharaoh, of his mother's hiding him in the little ark among the rushes in the river, and of his finding and adoption by Pharaoh's daughter, is an archetypal theme of the hero's birth and of the hatred generated in the collective mind by the appearance of the promise of individual consciousness. The hero's life is threatened as soon as he is born. He can only be saved at the outset if he is entrusted to the water, to the arms of the great maternal unconscious from which he must be reborn if he is to survive. Christ was saved from the slaughter of the Innocents by the *descent* into Egypt, a symbol of these depths.

The great value in each of us must be twice born. A new insight may be spontaneously, naturally born in any of us, but if we immediately expose it to the world and try to preach it or to live it outwardly in its infant stage, we will inevitably become identified with it, become personally inflated, and then be destroyed by the greed and envy of the collective shadow, the Herod within. Many writers have spoken of the absolute need to keep secret a new idea for a play or a book, for if it is exposed too soon, the inspiration will die. The revivalist preacher, filling vast auditoriums with hysterical followers, is another example of the man who has identified with a genuine insight and has destroyed it by declaring it to the world in its raw, unassimilated stage. The destruction may come about in any of these ways. The power goes out of the vision, or else we are delivered over to possession by the negative side of it. If it is to live, the new value must be given back to the unconscious at what seems like the risk of losing it. It must be constantly remembered. But it must be left alone to mature and grow until the time is ripe and it has transformed us from within so that we are strong enough to carry it in full consciousness before the world and to face the suffering it involves.

Moses had two mothers—three, really—his natural mother, Pharaoh's daughter, and the water of the river from which he was "drawn out." (The name *Moses* means "drawn out of the water.") Like the mothers of most men who come to greatness, Moses' mother was surely a remarkable woman; both his personal mothers seem to have had unusual qualities. His natural mother had the courage and intelligence to contrive her scheme to save him and to trust him to the water, whereupon he was given back to her to feed and nurse, but not to possess. If we will commit the inner child to the water, keep him hidden, let him go, then he is given back to us to nourish in secrecy but never to possess personally. Pharaoh's daughter in this context would be an image of the Self, the royal woman in the psyche of Moses' mother. Moses, thought of as the inner child of his mother, is nurtured both by his natural instinctive ties and by the great value of that which unites all opposites.

To return now to the young Moses himself, we may imagine him growing up in the luxury of Pharaoh's court but protected from it by his loyalty to his origins and by the nourishment that true feeling in the mother gives to the son. It is surely clear that both Pharaoh's daughter and his own mother loved him without possessiveness, that shadow side of a woman's feeling that kills all the true warmth of the heart. As we have seen, his natural mother had let him go, trusted him to the waters, and Pharaoh's daughter had the greatness of heart not to separate him from his roots, from his own people. How easy it would have been for her to bring him up in ignorance of who he was and whence he came, even in hatred of his own blood, since that must have been the acceptable attitude! There are many instances of this today—people bringing up their children to reject all that is dark and despised in themselves. We may imagine that Pharaoh's mother was both possessive and cold, spoiling him one moment, failing to discipline him the next, and encouraging an overwhelming sense of his own greatness.

Moses at first followed the conventional pattern for young men in his position, fighting with the army and proving himself as a man. He had probably always felt sorrow and pity for his people's plight, but it had not yet penetrated to his heart and made action imperative. It probably never occurred to him to become really involved until the day he killed the unjust overseer in a fit of furious anger. It was an impulsive, pointless killing, arousing hostility among the Hebrews themselves. Yet the chance of awakening comes almost always with a breakthrough of violent emotion, usually negative.

Moses must have seen at once that to meet crime with crime was no answer. In contrast to Pharaoh's reaction to such tests, he accepted responsibility for his shadow and the consequences of his act. He went into exile into Midian, there to spend long years in the search for discrimination, wisdom, and selflessness. As so often happens to all of us, it is the impulsive giving in to an emotional reaction, and the acceptance of full responsibility for it, which marks the beginning of reflection. Moses' fury sprang from the generous emotion of pity, but his action was merely a destructive release of his own painful feelings without objectivity or real compassion. Yet because of his integrity and willingness to pay the price, it must have marked for him the beginning of self-knowledge.

For Moses, as for all men, the conscious confrontation with the shadow was followed by the meeting with the *anima*, the finding of his individual feeling, his emotional freedom from the personal mother. As so often happens in the beautiful symbolism of the Old Testament, his *anima*, his future wife, comes to meet him at the well on the threshold of his new life in Midian. Surely in every true marriage the man meets the woman at the well, and she draws up water from the earth for him to drink. So also, inwardly, the *anima* in man draws water for him from the unconscious depths.

The seven daughters of Jethro, priest of the Midianites, are drawing water from the well, and Moses protects them from some rough shepherds who are interfering, thus rightly fulfilling his man's role as the women fulfill theirs. He is welcomed by Jethro into his house, marries his daughter, Zipporah, and settles down to the quiet life of a shepherd in the service of his father-in-law. At this point Moses probably envisaged his whole life as being spent in this uneventful, prosperous way. How very hard it must have been for this young man, an aristocrat by upbringing, a soldier who had dreamed of heroic exploits, no doubt, and whose warm heart and vivid imagination would keep alive in him the memory of his people's suffering! A hint of this is found in his cry when his son is born: "I am a stranger in a strange land" (Exod. 2:22). Yet he accepted without complaint the necessity of the long years of discipline.

With Moses, as with all of us, the turns of what seems like chance bring to us the exact situation in which we have the opportunity, if we will, to find the buried sides of our personality without which we can never live our true meaning as individuals; and usually the opportunity comes as a direct result of some major sin or failure of our earlier life. Moses' solitary life as a shepherd, the days and nights alone in the desert with his dog and his sheep, the gentle patience and skill so alien to his passionate nature (which he had to learn at lambing time), all these things nurtured the hitherto unlived potentialities of his psyche. Thus the door opened to the inner world; his ear opened to the voice of God in his heart; his eye opened to the vision of the divine. Imperceptibly, through the discipline of the daily simplicities, his shadow side was confronted, his sensitive individual feeling was discovered, and he came finally to so deep an awareness of the *Mysterium tremendum* that God spoke to him face to face.

The manner of the first vision, the breakthrough of the new consciousness in Moses that had been maturing for so long, is of great symbolic meaning. Moses' sin had arisen from a destructive feeling impulse that had possessed and blinded him. His vision of the burning bush was of a fire that burned but did not consume, out of which came the voice of God and the realization of his unique task as an individual. This is the moment of transformation. The intensity of the fire of natural instinct, never repressed or rejected, is transmuted through discipline and acceptance into the fire of creativity, which does not destroy but liberates. In Moses' case, this fire was powerful enough to liberate a whole nation from its slavery. The objectivity of real enthusiasm (which means "being filled with God") had taken the place of subjective anger.

We should not, however, make the common mistake of supposing that such an experience immediately rids the human personality of all its weaknesses and hesitations and that such a man has only to go forward in a state of detachment and certainty, freed once and for all from doubt and fear and anger. On the contrary, he has probably to carry a far greater burden of doubt and a more constant temptation from the shadow side than ever before. This was certainly so for Moses until the end of his life, and he remained altogether human in strength and in weakness through all the great events of which he was the instrument.

Almost always when such a moment comes to a man, he is

faced with the necessity of doing the very thing for which he is sure he has no natural gift, the thing he most fears. Moses had always been a man of action, but now he is told that he must go to Pharaoh and use *words*—that is, he must work through his inferior function, which, as Carl Jung says, is always the way of redemption. There are two ways in which we may evade this voice that commands us to enter the new way. We may become inflated with the power that now fills us, or we may take refuge in false humility. Moses is in danger of the latter. "Who am *I* that I should go unto Pharaoh?" he asks. "I am not eloquent; I am slow of speech, of a slow tongue; they will not believe me" (Exod. 3:11). But God rebukes Moses and tells him that Aaron, his brother, will go with him. (The necessary support from the "brother" without and within will be at hand.) God tells Moses to say that *I Am* has sent him. With the realization of the name of God, Moses cannot cling for long to his inferiority complex, which is the underside of inflation. Only true humility can bring the knowledge of this name. So Moses accepts his way and sets off on his journey back to Egypt.

Moses now carries out his task in the face of the grumbling disbelief of Israel. For Moses it is a time of preparation for leadership, for *doing the next thing* in obedience to the voice of God, without thought of risk and without discouragement. This is a stage we all know. We fail and fail and fail in our struggle with ourselves and must go on to the *next thing* until suddenly the moment of liberation comes. A transformation releases us from our conflict and we must make ready for the new journey. We must eat the Passover, the symbol of the crossing over into a new way of life. We must eat it standing, as did the Israelites, in complete readiness to seize the moment. In the exhilaration of freedom, we probably imagine that the land of milk and honey is just around the corner but, if so, we are soon disillusioned. There is a desert to be crossed—a long, austere journey through the dark and empty times that come to us after the old attitudes have been left behind and the new vision has been glimpsed but remains a hope unrealized.

Soon after the departure comes a moment of great danger. The pursuit by Pharaoh is the revenge of our old attitudes. They try to return and we have the feeling that we are shut in between mountain and sea. We can go neither forward nor back, and we are certain we shall be destroyed by the irresistible force of past habit and the overwhelming strength of collective reactions. It is a repetition of the theme of the newborn child threatened with extinction. Nothing we can humanly do or consciously decide will help us now. This is the moment at which only one kind of realization can save us; personal success or achievement, even in the realm of the spirit, must be seen as irrelevant. All that matters is that we have done our best; we have made the choice and eaten the Passover. Reason and will can do no more, and we entrust the "new child" to the water again. Moses knows this. He does not panic, for he has heard the name of God, and behold, the wind of the spirit begins to blow over the sea. There is a meeting of wind and water, of spirit and instinct, a mighty, creative moment. The water is blown back, a clear path ahead is opened for Moses and his people, and when they have passed over, the same wind and water swallow up and destroy the power of the old attitudes. We are set free to grow if we will. The children of Israel can move on to Sinai, to the holy mountain where Moses again meets God, face to face, and brings down to the people the covenant and the law.

A beautiful incident worth recounting happens before Moses and his people reach Sinai. Jethro, Moses' father-in-law, comes from Midian to meet Moses. We feel the love between them and the wisdom of the old man. Moses has been making the usual mistake of the man of good will who takes on a tremendous responsibility. He is trying to carry the burden on the *wrong level.* Every day he sits from morning to evening hearing the problems of the people, settling individual disputes, until he is weary to the point of collapse. With wise common sense, Jethro tells Moses that he must appoint elders for this task; Moses himself must deal only with the questions of vital importance. If he continues to wear himself out in this way, he will have no energy left for maintaining the contact with God, the vital spark in the hearts of the people that alone can bring them to their goal. Only so can he carry the weight of his vocation. Moses accepts Jethro's insights immediately and with humility.

Moses now ascends the mountain and once more meets God face to face. He hides his face before the glory of this vision. He cannot bear more than a glimpse, but the glimpse has transformed him. When he comes down from the mountain, his face is shining with so great a light that he must wear a veil over it, for there are things that cannot be borne by unconscious people, which must be hidden for their sake. T. S. Eliot wrote that human beings cannot stand very much reality. Moses has spent forty days and forty nights alone on Horeb. During this time he has not only come to his great inner vision, but he has also understood many things of an entirely practical nature. The truly great mystic, contrary to popular belief, is not someone floating on a cloud, detached from outer reality; on the contrary, the mystic has a far better grasp of the essentials in human affairs than the busy man or woman of action.

Moses now knows the necessity for the laws whereby a society must be held together, the essential disciplines that the unconscious individual must accept from without if he is ever to grow to self-discipline. He also brings down from the mountain plans for the building of the Ark, for he understands the immense importance of ritual, of the symbols essential to maintaining contact with the inner meaning of one's life. If Moses needed confirmation of this importance, he found it when he returned to his people from the mountain. During his long absence, they had been unable to retain the sense of meaning that he personally embodied and carried for them. They had made a golden calf and projected all their unconscious needs onto this idol.

When Moses discovers his people's golden calf, he furiously hurls to the ground the tables of stone on which the law was written, breaking them to pieces. Yahweh is equally angry, but Moses recollects his humility and stands between his people and the wrath of God, the revenge of the unconscious forces. Yahweh's anger is turned away and the tables of the law are restored.

Later on, when the children of Israel have refused their first chance to enter Canaan and Yahweh has said to Moses, "I will disinherit them and make *thee* a greater nation" (Num. 14:12), Moses does not falter. He does not abandon his people, who, while depending on him, constantly abused him and cursed him for bringing them away from the fleshpots of Egypt. It is often a very great temptation for a man or woman of great understanding to say, "Why bother anymore with these people who are so blind? God is doing great things in *me;* these others are hopeless."

The Psalmist wrote of the children of Israel, "He [Yahweh] would have destroyed them, had not Moses, his chosen, stood before him in the gap to turn away his wrathful indignation" (Ps. 106:23). In every age there are people like Moses who "stand in the gap"—poets, artists, men of vision, who bridge the widening split between conscious and unconscious, between darkness and light—mediators without whom the opposites would fly apart to the ultimate destruction of humanity.

Moses refused personal glorification; he refused to identify his ego with his vision of God, to become a *Fuehrer,* a *Duce.* He retained the essential humility of the true leader and guide. The incident of Joshua's protest when he found two men "prophesying" in the camp shows this beautiful quality in Moses. He replied to Joshua's anger at the thought that anyone other than Moses should presume to prophesy: "Enviest thou for my sake? Would God that *all* the Lord's people were prophets and that the Lord would put his spirit upon them" (Num. 11:29).

Moses also knew how to accept help. In battle he needed two men to hold up his arms because he was so weary. In moments of danger we are arrogant indeed if we will not recognize our need for those who will "hold up our arms."

Moses' weaknesses are never glossed over. They are seen clearly, even as an essential ingredient of human greatness. He had moments of great despondency in those forty years of unremitting labor. At one of these times God appointed seventy elders to help him. "They shall bear the burden of these people with thee" (Num. 11:17). Help came at all these times.

There was, however, one moment when Moses fell seriously into possession by his old angry shadow, in spite of all his wisdom and humility. The children of Israel were grumbling and complaining because there was no water. As usual, they blamed it on Moses, forgetting all the proofs of God's protection that had been given to them. God told Moses to "speak to the rock" and ask it to give forth water, but Moses was less patient than Yahweh this time. He lost his temper, just as he had lost it so many years ago in his youth when he killed the overseer. "Hear now ye rebels," he said, "must we fetch you water out of that rock?" (Num. 20:10) And he struck the rock in anger and the water gushed out. He was guilty of a major sin—discourtesy to God, to man, and to matter. In *hubris* he identified with God. "Must *we* fetch you water . . . ?" He spoke to his fellow Israelites with contempt, a very different thing from healthy anger, and he struck the rock with violence instead of with respect.

It is said by the chronicles that for this sin God forbade Moses himself to go into the promised land. Power that is not relinquished at the right moment can be a very great danger, not only for the one who wields it, but for his or her followers also. If Moses had gone into the new land with his people, the projection upon him would have been so great that it would have been almost impossible for Moses to resist identifying with the personal love of power that was a characteristic of his shadow. The danger from the shadow becomes greater, not less, for such a man, and by the deepest paradox, he is saved at the high point of achievement by the shadow itself. If Moses had not fallen into the sin of striking the rock, he would never have realized that the moment had come for him to renounce his leadership, and a subtle corruption would have begun.

In *The Lord of the Rings* it is Gollum who saves Frodo at his supreme moment, when he falls under the power of the Ring on the very brink of success. If Frodo himself had thrown the ring into the fire, he would almost certainly have identified with his heroic role. He might have lost his humanity and have begun another reign of power in the world. So always must a person's salvation come in the supreme moment, after the long purging, from beyond the ego.

If Moses had gone into Canaan with the children of Israel, they would have continued in a state of childish dependency and refusal of adult responsibility. Moses, accepting his sin, his humanity, darkness and light, was now freed from the final danger and the "promised land" was no longer a goal, but a fact of the spirit. He went up into the mountain, looked on the new world he had opened for his people, and died in the fullness of wisdom.

The Children of Israel

Moses and Pharaoh are the images of the hero and the renegade, but the story of the children of Israel is the story of the ordinary person who inwardly carries both these images, responding first to one and then to the other. This ordinary person instinctively knows that beyond the opposites of hero and renegade there is harmony and an answer to all questionings, and so he or she continues to stumble along toward the promised land.

The Hebrews were enslaved in Egypt just as we all are enslaved in different ways—by our blindness, our identification with collective attitudes, our clinging to one kind of safety or another. Sooner or later this darkness is suddenly broken by a glimpse of freedom, usually coming to us, as it did to the children of Israel, through contact with a free person, a Moses. Such a person fires a spark in us, by the light of which we know for a moment the potential Moses in ourselves, the possibility of becoming a free and aware person. The glimpse, the momentary enthusiasm, brings with it almost at once a resistance, for we know instinctively what it is going to cost us if we consent to recognize the Moses within. The Pharaoh in us is increased in strength by the threat to his "domination," so we begin to make excuses. The children of Israel, rejoicing at Moses' first message, turned against him again as soon as they felt Pharaoh's increased oppression. Great as their sufferings were, they had at first an even greater fear of the unknown. When we do finally consent to face the unknown and confront Pharaoh, our shadow side, it appears incomprehensible that for so long we preferred to stay in "Egypt," tormented by the meaningless horrors of neurotic suffering, rather than endure the truth about ourselves. But at first we cling desperately to our neurosis as to a lifeline. To let it go feels like letting go of one's identity because it means an end to identification with our particular cherished image of ourselves.

Suffering of the Hebrews had grown so great, however, that when Moses bade them be ready on the Passover night, one and all were obedient, and the greater journey began. The Pharaoh within is defeated for the moment—and this is the crucial moment for the children of Israel, just as there always comes a crucial choice for an individual. It is the crisis at which a "no" is fatal, but a "yes" means a fundamental choice of direction. The weaknesses that lead to all the ups and downs and regressions of daily living do not, except in cases of real, conscious betrayal, alter this direction, though they increase the length of the journey.

The Egyptians have loaded the Israelites with presents to speed their going. In addition, the Israelites have taken all the gold and precious things they can lay hands on, for the Egyptians are too terrified to resist. The first effort toward freedom is usually accompanied by a kind of greed, the nature of freedom being very dimly understood. At this point it is merely a promise of release from old kinds of suffering. "Immediate" wealth is demanded and, for a brief time, experienced.

No sooner, however, have the Israelites set out than Moses reveals to them the price they must pay. The angel of death, which killed the firstborn, has passed them over because they have heard the voice of God and are willing to face the unknown wilderness. But that which happens disastrously and meaninglessly to people who refuse consciousness must also be experienced by the "chosen" freely and willingly. Every man of the Hebrews must dedicate his firstborn son to the service of God. Here is the symbol that carries the meaning of true freedom. Only that person is free who can willingly and gladly submit to another kind of bond. The firstborn, the heir, is the greatest value, that which carries the essential meaning of our personality and its creativity. To dedicate this to God means to let go of all our possessiveness, our stake in our achievements, our sense of personal "rights," our conscious assumptions that we are owed a return for effort. Only when we have learned through our forty years in the wilderness to *choose necessity* with absolutely no reservation do we come to the truth that makes us free.

What a shock to the children of Israel, congratulating themselves on their chosen state, rejoicing in their plunder and their escape from bondage! Probably, however, few of them realized at this point that the "sacrifice of the son" represented more than a special kind of life for their eldest boy, or recognized it as a hint of the long and agonizing process of purging hidden from them, as it is mercifully hidden from us when we begin the journey.

At the first major setback between the mountains and the Red Sea, the Hebrews are rudely awakened from their dream of a quick triumphal procession to the land of milk and honey. Pharaoh is not to be thrown off so easily. We find that the old habits of bondage are immensely strong. The first upsurge of enthusiasm recedes and the chariots and horses of the old way of life, the old easy attitudes, come galloping after us. There is no escape. The unconscious is silent; conscious resolutions to change are of no avail. We begin to grumble, to accuse the "Moses" within, and also our friends (upon whom he is projected) for having brought us to this impasse. Maybe we have made some big change in our outer life, expecting a new and satisfying experience, and all it has brought us is a feeling of a dead end. We don't even have the old sense of safety in bondage; will we listen to Moses or go down under Pharaoh? Maybe it is in this moment that we fully realize that "Moses" has offered us "blood, toil, sweat, and tears," not a quick, easy way to marvelous inner experiences. We know for a moment a full acceptance of this way. This is indeed the crucial moment. If we say "yes" to it, the wind of God blows back the waters so that we may make that essential crossing over from the old to the new way, and Pharaoh and his might are swallowed up behind us. We have made the fundamental choice of direction, which frees us, not from the long journey with its many backslidings, but from the danger of complete regression through a weak discouragement, which can kill us at this point. It is a far worse danger than it was before the Passover because the new way has been glimpsed and we have actually set foot upon it. If we hold firm and cross over to the other side out of Egypt, the end is no longer in doubt, however long delayed, unless we deliberately, and with full consciousness of what we are doing, betray and deny our original choice. (This is the Church's definition of mortal sin.)

The sea is crossed and the journey proper begins. There is now a visible guiding symbol—the pillar of cloud and of fire. In the daytime, in the light of extraverted life, it is a cloudy, indistinct thing, but it is nevertheless unquestionably real. At night in dreams, in introversion, it burns with a clear light. The multitude, weighted down with all their possessions, travels slowly and soon runs out of food. For the first time the so often repeated cry is heard: "Why did you bring us out of Egypt? At least we had enough to eat there." The answer, not because they *deserved* it, but because the "Moses" within them did not lose faith and courage, was the manna that fed them unfailingly through the coming forty years.

The manna is a small, round, colorless thing lying on our doorstep, so to speak, to be had for the picking up. Its peculiarity is that we cannot hoard it; it is food for one day only. Each day, if we are to have strength to continue the journey, it must be picked up. This much effort only is required. There is no *kick* to this basic nourishment. It has little taste or savor. Perhaps these qualities symbolize the day-to-day picking up of the most ordinary colorless tasks that every human being must face and "eat"—that is, *accept.* The manna is the essential food for the journey. The Host in the Mass, the bread from heaven, is an ordinary, tasteless fragment of daily bread transformed by its conscious "lifting up" into the body of Christ—the essential incarnate essence of truth, of the Self. So the Hebrews, by simply picking up and eating what was there in abundance all around them, unearned, unsought for, were fed and nourished on the journey.

Fairly soon, however, the Hebrews got bored with this daily, tasteless food which did not leave them with lovely feelings or titillate their appetites. They demanded flesh to eat. And because they were weak and could not get along without some external "kicks," God sent them quails. The Psalmist says, "Lust came upon them in the wilderness and they tempted God in the desert. And he gave them their desire and sent leanness withal into their soul" (Ps. 106:14–15). We always get what we really want, although we may seldom recognize it as the thing we think we want. It is most certain that every demand for personal power or satisfaction is immediately counterbalanced by a leanness of soul. That is not to say that the good things of the flesh are not to be enjoyed to the full. It is no long-faced puritanical denial of instinct and the beauty of good food and wine and so on. It is a matter of the *demand* for such things at the expense of or to the exclusion of greater values. Still more, it is a symbol of the lust for spiritual power, the clinging to lofty feelings, which is much more intoxicating than wine. These demands make us fat and comfortable in one sense and induce an exactly corresponding leanness and starvation in the innermost places of the soul.

After they have arrived at the holy mountain, the Hebrews are in for a long delay. It seems at this stage on the journey that "Moses," the spark that leads, is no longer visible. We know in our heads that he has only receded out of our awareness and is gathering strength in the depths—or on the heights of the mountain—to lead us farther, but gradually we forget and lose faith and end in a panic, looking for other gods—gods we can see and touch, or easier concepts of an all-powerful anthropomorphic deity who will make us feel safe and answer our immediate prayers. Even Aaron (the "priest" in us, who is closest to Moses and is his brother) breaks faith and serves the collective panic. They make a god out of the gold, the values they have brought from Egypt, a golden calf, a bull, the symbol of unbridled instinct.

After such a fall we must be ruthless with ourselves. Moses causes the ringleaders to be killed; we may have to cut out of our lives many things, even relationships, which have hitherto seemed natural and pleasant but have lost their meaning. This letting go of things would, however, be pointless asceticism if, at the same time, we did not pour the energy released from the "golden calf" into new channels of creation. Moses immediately set the Israelites to work on the building of the tabernacle. In their repentance and new humility they made free gifts of the treasures they had brought from Egypt for the creation of the beautiful symbol of their deepest faith—the Ark of the Covenant. The actual building of the Ark was carried out by those who had proved themselves "wise hearted." So, if we listen and pay the price, the wisdom of the inner world will create for us the symbols whereby we may hold to the meaning of our journey.

After only two or three years in the wilderness, the Israelites come to the borders of the promised land, and Moses sends out scouts into Canaan. When they return with their reports, all but two are frightened and urge the people not to risk entering the country. Only Joshua and Caleb are for the bold course, but the children of Israel will not listen to them and fall into an ugly panic, abusing Moses as usual and demanding another leader to take them back to Egypt. It is a major refusal and must be bitterly paid for.

It must be remembered that at this stage of the journey a refusal is a very different thing from the weak backslidings of the beginning. This conscious turning back is a betrayal of their quest, and in rage Yahweh condemns them to wander long years in the wilderness. Their children will enter the promised land; they will not. Only Joshua and Caleb are excepted. The people now repent under this threat and insist upon going out and fighting a battle with the Canaanites in spite of Moses' warning. "The Lord is not among you," he says, for they are acting out of fear, not faith. They are defeated and the years of wandering begin. It seems a harsh punishment, but there are indeed moments in the life of an individual when a refusal such as this is irreversible without long years of suffering, perhaps even for the rest of this mortal life, in which case it will mean that the children must pick up the burden of the unlived lives of their fathers or mothers, and to them also in due time will come the moment of the great choice on the threshold of the holy land.

The Bacchae, by Euripides

T*he Bacchae* was one of Euripides' three last plays, probably written after he was exiled from Athens at the age of 70 in 408 B.C.[1] William Arrowsmith, in the introduction to his translation of the play, writes, "It is, clearly and flatly, that unmistakable thing, a masterpiece; a play which, for dramatic turbulence and comprehensiveness and the sheer power of its poetry, is unmatched by any except the greatest among ancient and modern tragedies. . . . Elusive, complex and compelling, the play constantly recedes before one's grasp, advancing, not retreating, steadily into deeper chaos and larger order, coming finally to rest God knows where—which is to say, where it matters" (p. 344).

These words echo H. C. Goddard's thoughts about *King Lear.* He, too, urges each individual reader to surrender himself to the play, to dare to plunge in his imagination into the "deeper chaos" and to find the "larger order." It is the fire of each reader's own imagination responding to that of the poet that will yield the meaning so that he or she may come "to rest God knows where . . . where it matters."

---

[1] The edition used is *The Complete Greek Tragedies,* vol. 7, Euripides III, ed. David Grene and Richmond Lattimore (Chicago: The University of Chicago Press, 1960). The passages cited from William Arrowsmith's version of Euripides' *Bacchae* form part of a *verse* translation which has here to our regret and the translator's dismay been reduced to prose.

The myth of Dionysus, which provides the theme of the play, tells how Semele, daughter of the old King Cadmus of Thebes, and sister of Agave, the mother of Pentheus, was with child by her union with Zeus; how Hera, Zeus' wife, discovered the pregnancy and, in her jealous rage, persuaded Semele to beg Zeus to show himself to her in his true form; how Zeus foolishly consented, and Semele was consumed by the lightning of the god whom no human being may look upon and live. Zeus, however, snatched the child from the ashes, and cutting open his thigh, hid the premature baby therein, sewing up the cavity until it was time for him to be born. Thus Dionysus was born first from his mother's womb and second from the womb of his divine father's thigh. Semele's sisters, however, refused to believe any of this, saying that Semele and Cadmus had made it up to hide the shame of her illegitimate pregnancy. Thus the divinity of Dionysus was denied in Thebes.

The story of the young Dionysus' death and dismemberment at the hands of the Titans and of his restoration to life is not explicitly mentioned in this play, but is reflected in the dismemberment of Pentheus. It is important to remember that Dionysus was the dying and rising god of the Greeks and that his cult was a dark mystery religion, alien to the conscious thinking and to the rational, daylight worship of the Olympians. He was associated with the Eleusinian mysteries and was the masculine counterpart of Persephone. (He was sometimes called Bromios.) It is a fact that his rites returned to Greece from the East and that their wilder and more savage aspects were transformed by the Greeks into controlled ecstasy. We may be reminded of the end of Aeschylus' *Oresteia*, when the Furies, the ancient goddesses of the dark, bent on destruction because of their long rejection by men, are reconciled by Athene's recognition of their validity and of their power to bless as well as to destroy.

In the *Bacchae* the chorus of Asian women whom Dionysus has brought with him from the East sings of the possibility of the union of opposites. In this union ecstasy, the intoxication of the god, ceases to be a violent swing from the heights of religious feeling to the depths of instinctive savagery. Though they sing of the possibility, the women themselves remain ambivalent. Only at the end does Euripedes lead us to the "place that matters," in which there is no denial of the god, yet no possession by the god. It is only through the compassion of the human heart that the duality of the archetypes may be transcended. But before we reach this place, Euripides forces us to look without illusion into the terrible extremes of beauty and horror to which the mighty power of the god can lead us.

Four different kinds of reaction to the impact of Dionysus are shown in the play, and their consequences are ruthlessly laid bare. First, the Asian women of the chorus come nearest, until the last scene, to a conscious relationship to the god, though in spite of their vision they sometimes fall into violent hatred. Second, the old men, Cadmus (the former king, father of Semele and of Agave, in favor of whose son, Pentheus, he has abdicated) and Teiresias (the blind seer), both give pious and rationalized lip service to the god without any real involvement. They take out insurance policies, as it were. Third, the women of Thebes, led by Agave and her sisters, are possessed by the god in the unconscious and rush into the hills at the mercy of the positive and negative poles of the ecstasy. And fourth, the young king Pentheus is completely skeptical, determined to stamp out all this irrational wilderness by force and establish the sole supremacy of cool reason and common sense. Thus he falls helplessly into the power of the god, is completely overwhelmed, and is led inevitably to a horrible death.

The play opens with the god Dionysus alone on the stage beside the tomb of his mother, Semele, in Thebes. Disguised as a man, he describes in a long speech the death of his mother by the fire of Zeus, his father, his present return to Thebes from his journeyings in the East, and his intention to prove his divinity to the people and to the king, Pentheus, by driving the women of the city into the hills in mad ecstasy.

The chorus of women from the east now enters, singing of the god and of the joy of his worship. They are dressed in fawn skins, crowned with ivy and snakes, and each holds a *thyrsus*, the holy wand of the god. Dionysus was the god of all growing things (not only of the vine), and wherever he walked there came a burst of vegetation. So also in the human psyche that yielded to him there came an uprush of instinctive energy, the activation of the animal psyche, an ecstasy of the body driving the worshipper to run, to leap, to mate, to hunt, and to kill—but also to dance.

"Blessed is he," sings the chorus, "who hallows his life in the worship of god, he whom the spirit of god possesseth, who is one with those who belong to the holy body of god. Blessed are the dancers and those who are purified, who dance on the hill in the holy dance of god" (p. 362). The implication is clear—the dance has been from the most primitive times the symbolic living of the wild, instinctive energy in human beings. It both arouses this energy and may purify it. The uncontrollable life force is given a form, a pattern, a meaning. We may still say with the women of the chorus, "Blessed are the dancers, for they are purified." Possession may become worship in the dance, whether it is an actual physical dance or the "dance" we express in poetry, in fantasy, in painting, in music, in true play, or in an activity of the creative imagination, for the dance was the original art, the mother of all the others. All true rituals are a kind of dance; the Mass itself is still recognizably so.

Civilized humankind imagines that these instinctive ecstasies may be safely dispensed with, so they sink into the unconscious, where they turn destructive. Even the safety valves of which Alan McGlashan speaks in *The Savage and Beautiful Country*, such as Carnival, are seldom available today and are losing their ritual meaning. And so we dance together in this way no longer, and the frenzy of the god breaks out in violence and in war.

Each individual, then, must reach down alone to the ecstasy and find her or his own "dance," her or his own creative activity through which she or he consciously enters the great dance of the world. The springing up everywhere of groups in which people let loose their emotions together is surely a symptom of the desperate need for a safety valve. As such they may be of great value for the relief of pressure, but unless there is a transcending image, a symbol creating a sense of awe, something that turns the outpouring of emotions into a "dance," they remain simply a *safety* measure, powerless to alter either an individual or society. The experience of the unconscious without discipline and hard work ends up as meaningless.

The long and hauntingly beautiful hymn of praise to the god sung by the chorus is followed by the entry of the two old men. The contrast is startling. Teiresias begins by talking about the agreement the two have made in cold blood to "dress in skins of fawn and crown our heads with ivy" (p. 365). Both are bent with age and talk of going to the mountain and treading the dance of the god to forget their age. It is pathetic and incongruous. Teiresias says, "We are the heirs of customs and traditions hallowed by age and handed down to us by our fathers. . . ." (p. 367). Since the god desires to be honored by all, he continues, they will go and dance too. They miss the point entirely. The dead hand of tradition is upon them, and they can conceive of the dance of the god only in an outer sense. Both great men in their youth, their vision has atrophied. They have not withdrawn their projections to find the god within. Thus they have become frozen in tradition, doing what is expected of them for safety's sake.

Teiresias had been a prophet and a seer, and it is clear that his gift has deserted him and that he is trying to reestablish himself, extolling this new god. In a long, highly rational speech about the power of the god, he upbraids Pentheus for his disbelief. He interprets the story of the thigh of Zeus by saying it was the misunderstanding of a word that led the people to believe in it. Nothing could more clearly show his loss of vision than this descent from the intuitive understanding of myth to a sterile, intellectual juggling with words. Cadmus supports him with a more openly cynical attitude. "Even if this Dionysus is no god, as you assert," he says to Pentheus, "persuade yourself that he is. The fiction is a noble one, for Semele will seem to be the mother of a god, and this confers no small distinction on our family" (p. 372). Reading this speech, we feel far more sympathy for

Pentheus in his blind but honestly violent reaction than for these "sensible" old men.

We turn now to the women, the *Bacchae*, who, although they do not actually appear on the stage, are the power behind the entire action, the cause, inner and outer, of all that happens. The long-rejected feminine values have broken out of the unconscious in a wild burst of instinctive energy. From the beginning to the end of the play, though unseen, they are vividly alive in our imagination. Let us listen to the description of the messenger who brings news of what is going on to Pentheus:

> About that hour when the sun lets loose its light to warm the earth our grazing herds of cows had just begun to climb the path along the mountain ridge. Suddenly I saw three companies of dancing women. . . . There they lay in the deep sleep of exhaustion, some resting on boughs of fir, others sleeping where they fell, here and there among the oak leaves—but all modestly and soberly, not, as you think, drunk with wine, nor wandering, led astray by the music of the flute, to hunt their Aphrodite through the woods.
>
> But your mother heard the lowing of our horned herds, and springing to her feet, gave a great cry to waken them from sleep. And they too, rubbing the blossom of soft sleep from their eyes, rose up lightly and straight—a lovely sight to see: all as one, the old women and the young and the unmarried girls. First they let their hair fall loose, down over their shoulders, and those whose straps had slipped fastened their skins of fawn with writhing snakes that licked their cheeks. Breasts swollen with milk, new mothers who had left their babies behind at home nestled gazelles and young wolves in their arms suckling them. They crowned their hair with leaves—ivy and oak and flowering bryony. One woman struck her thyrsus against a rock and a fountain of cool water came bubbling up. Another drove her fennel in the ground, and where it struck the earth, at the touch of god, a spring of wine poured out. Those who wanted milk scratched at the soil with bare fingers and the white milk came welling up. If you had been there and seen these wonders for

yourself you would have gone down on your knees yourself and prayed to the god you now deny. (pp. 388–89)

And now we hear what happens when this extreme is *attacked*
by its opposite—not confronted, as Athene confronted the
Furies, but attacked by ego-inspired reason.

We cowherds and shepherds gathered in small groups,
wondering and arguing among ourselves at these fantas-
tic things. But then a city fellow with the knack of words
rose to his feet and said: "All who live upon the pastures
of the mountain, what do you say? Shall we earn a little
favor with King Pentheus by hunting his mother Agave
out of the revels?" Falling in with his suggestion we
withdrew and set ourselves in ambush, hidden by the
leaves among the undergrowth. Then at a signal all the
Bacchae whirled their wands for the revels to begin.
With one voice they cried aloud: "O Bacchos, Son of
Zeus! O Bromios," they cried until the beasts and all the
mountain seemed wild with divinity. . . .
It happened, however, that Agave ran near the ambush
where I lay concealed. Leaping up, I tried to seize her,
but she gave a cry: "Hounds who run with the men are
hunting us down. Follow, follow me. Use your wands for
weapons!" At this we fled and barely missed being torn to
pieces by the women. Unarmed they swooped down
upon the herds of cattle grazing there on the green of the
meadow. And then you could have seen a single woman
with bare hands tear a fat calf, still bellowing with fright,
in two, while others clawed the heifers to pieces—and
bulls, their raging fury gathered in their horns, lowered
their heads to charge, then fell, stumbling, to the earth,
pulled down by hordes of women and stripped of flesh
and skin more quickly, sire, than you could blink your
royal eyes. (pp. 389–90)

Notice that it is a "city fellow" with a knack of words who is
the cause of this change. The brief phrase evokes a picture of the
superficialities of a one-sidedly masculine civilization, with its
rejection of the wordless power of nature, of all the values of

Eros. The "city fellow" is possessed by words and the desire for gain, the women are possessed by the numinous forces of the unconscious. In neither is there any *human* feeling. The mothers have left their human children at home and are suckling animals. The peasant messenger, however, has learned a lesson and in his simple way grasps that conscious acceptance of the god is the answer. He urges the king to recognize this, saying, "If there is no god of wine [of irrational inspiration, that is], there is no love" (p. 391).

Pentheus' reply is total rejection. "Like a blazing fire this Bacchic violence spreads. It comes too close. We are disgraced, humiliated in the eyes of Hellas. There is no time for hesitation" (p. 391). He orders out all his troops to attack the women. He will meet violence with violence. Reason is *humiliated* by instinct, and Pentheus has no gift of imagination, through which alone can come the reconciliation. How often do we do just this, in large things and in small, when we feel disgraced and humiliated by some outburst of irrational instinct that seizes us so that we are "not ourselves." We either force it out of sight as quickly as possible or we allow it to swamp us, so that we wallow in depression and remorse rather than make the painful effort of *imaginative* (not theoretical) understanding. It is the same thing in reverse, of course, when those who rightly rebel against conventional rationality exalt the instinctive reaction as the only value.

Pentheus refuses the warning of his first confrontation with Dionysus. He is a young man to be arrested and thrown into prison. But before he does this, he questions the disguised god and their brief exchange of words lays bare the impossibility of direct communication between the rational and the mystical. Pentheus' questions are all beside the point.

PENTHEUS: What form do they take, these mysteries of yours?
DIONYSUS: It is forbidden to tell the uninitiate.
PENTHEUS: Tell me the benefits that those who know your mysteries enjoy. [How familiar this question!]

DIONYSUS: I am forbidden to say. But they are worth knowing.
PENTHEUS: Your answers are designed to make me curious.
DIONYSUS: No. Our mysteries abhor an unbelieving man. . . .
PENTHEUS: Do you hold your rites during the day or night?
DIONYSUS: Mostly by night. The darkness is well suited to devotion.
PENTHEUS: Better suited to lechery and to seducing women.
DIONYSUS: You can find debauchery by daylight, too.
PENTHEUS: You shall regret these clever answers.
DIONYSUS: And you your stupid blasphemies. (pp. 376–379)

The truth that a man who lives entirely by rational values is as debauched in mind as one given over wholly to instinct is debauched in body is simply inconceivable to a Pentheus. The whole of this conversation could be translated with very little change into an exchange between a bigoted materialist and a convinced believer today.

Dionysus warns Pentheus that he is heading for trouble if he tries to shut him up in prison, for he *cannot* be confined. Indeed, he cannot—then or now. Pentheus now takes a step fatal to himself. He cuts off Dionysus' hair, calling it "girlish." This act symbolizes his determination to drain the feminine side of *himself* of all power. He takes into his own hand the god's wand, symbol of authority, and so commits himself to the terrible course of playing god, the end of which is inevitable disaster. "You take it. It belongs to Dionysus," says Dionysus ominously. "You do not know the limits of your strength. You do not know what to do. You do not know who you are." This is the truth that the *hubris* of conscious reason will not hear.

Dionysus is imprisoned and there comes an earthquake and a thunderbolt from heaven, setting fire again to the tomb of Semele and destroying the whole palace of Pentheus. Dionysus reappears, reassuring his frightened women from Asia, and tells them of the attempt to bind him.

"He seemed to think he was chaining me but never once so much as touched my hands. He *fed on his desires*. . . . Inside the stable he intended as my jail, instead of me, he found a bull and tried to rope its knees and hooves. He was panting desperately, biting his lips with his teeth, his whole body drenched with sweat, while I sat nearby, quietly watching" (p. 385).

Attempting to do the impossible, bind the god, Pentheus does not even see that he is binding his own bull, symbol of his own masculine instinctive strength.

We remember this image when Dionysus and Pentheus again confront each other after Pentheus has ordered out his army to round up the women. This is his last blustering and empty gesture of masculinity, which has already become dependent on the collective army. He has indeed succeeded in binding his bull, and we now watch him surrendering in the most abject way to the power of the god via the inevitable *enantiodromia,* the turning of his rejection of the feminine values into an identification with an inferior femininity.

The unconscious will always give repeated warnings to such a man, through dreams, through the words of others, through the shock of catastrophe, perhaps. So Pentheus is warned over and over again by the god, by his elders, by the chorus, by his own servants, and finally by his failure to "bind" the god, to silence the voice of the unconscious. The fire and earthquake have no influence either, for rationalism, which believes dogmatically in cause and effect, is blind to the identity of the inner and outer worlds.

> DIONYSUS: Pentheus, you do not hear, or else you disregard my words of warning. You have done me wrong, and yet, in spite of that, I warn you once again: do not take arms against a god. Stay quiet here. (p. 392)

Pentheus scoffs at this, and Dionysus makes one last try. He says he will bring the women peacefully home if only Pentheus will stay quiet. There follows Pentheus' final refusal. It is impossible for such a man to believe that if only he will stay quiet, do nothing, the unconscious will solve his problem. We all know this from bitter experience. Our deep-rooted belief that only by

action can we accomplish anything dies very hard and we have
to be aware of it every day—asserting and reasserting the value
of keeping still, doing nothing (which is not at all the same thing
as being idle, or withdrawing from life).

It is at this point of ultimate rejection that Pentheus inevitably delivers himself over to the power of the god, and having refused to be *still* becomes instead wholly passive—and that
power that had offered him life and understanding turns into a
cunning, destructive force leading him to final disaster. "This is
some trap," is Pentheus' reply to Dionysus' offer of help. "Bring
my armour, someone. And you *stop* talking" (p. 393).

The next scene is an extraordinarily vivid and terrible picture
of how one's attitude to the archetype is that which determines
its positive or negative power in one's life. Pentheus refuses to
hear the *word* and so he is delivered over to words. He believes it
a *trap* when the voice from the unconscious offers salvation
through humility, and so the same voice proceeds indeed to trap
him by urging him to set a trap for others. All that remains of
true discrimination regresses into cunning, into a despicable sort
of curiosity. It is not long before he is consenting to wear
women's clothes, his boasted strength of mind is entirely gone,
and the unconscious floods in, possessing him, forcing him back
into the infantile psyche, into the arms of the mother who will
finally destroy him.

This scene, with its almost unbearably painful double mean-
ings, leads us inexorably on to an ever deeper realization of the
horror of possession by an archetype. It is here that we plunge
indeed into the "deeper chaos." Yet there is a terrifying order in
it all, the absolutely cold logic of each extreme precisely repro-
ducing its opposite whenever the human heart and the human
imagination are silent. Every detail of the previous confrontation between Dionysus and Pentheus, and all Pentheus' blind reactions in the earlier scene, are played upon by the god and
turned into the means of the king's destruction. His repressed
curiosity about the women's doings is brought to fever heat. He
is led cunningly to the point of disguising himself in women's

clothes—of wearing a wig resembling the "girlish curls" he had cut off Dionysus' head in contempt. The thyrsus he had stolen from Dionysus is put into his hands. Then, when Pentheus returns to the stage dressed as a woman, coy and fussing about his appearance ("Do I look like my mother?" he asks) he sees Dionysus for a moment as a bull. This is to say that the bull he tried to bind is now filled with numinous power over him, as are all rejected things. The pitiless logic is complete. The superhuman god possesses the subhuman man, and this is hell. The women are behaving like animals, Pentheus is behaving like a god, and human kindness is completely swallowed up.

As we read this scene it is easy, however much we may be moved by its horror, to evade its application to ourselves. This is an extreme situation, though perhaps not so rare as we may imagine, but day by day we are all in some way possessed by this god or by that, calling these gods by their modern names of complex, mood, depression, inflation, and so on. To the exact degree that we despise and reject a fact or a feeling, to the same exact degree are we blindly possessed by that very thing.

We are told now by a messenger of the ghastly happenings on the mountain. The women have returned to their innocuous play after the wildness induced by the "city fellow." We may identify with one side of the psyche peacefully and happily *for a certain time;* that is to say, until a challenge comes from the other side. Until Dionysus came to Thebes, Pentheus was no doubt a just and able ruler, upholding the laws, kind and reasonable. We have no feeling that he was corrupt or cruel. Similarly, the women, left to themselves, indulged in no orgies, either of sex or of killing, and simply played happily in the woods "frisking like fillies newly freed from the painted bridles," says the messenger. But such a state of happy identification *invites* its opposite, and inevitably in everyone's life, the challenge comes. Pentheus arrives, eager to see the orgies his heated unconscious has been imagining while he was consciously spurning them. Dionysus, bending a tall fir tree down, seats Pentheus at the crest and then lets it rise above the other trees, and the women see him. A voice cries "Avenge yourselves on him that mocked your mysteries." "Maddened by the breath of the god," they rush to dislodge him with stones and finally with superhuman strength tear the fir tree from the ground, and Pentheus falls. His own mother, Agave, seizes him as a priestess does her victim. Pentheus tears off his wig, now crying to her to recognize him, begging for that humanity which he had forsworn. "Pity me, spare me, Mother! I have done a wrong, but do not kill your own son" (p. 407). It is too late. She is blind and deaf in her frenzy, hears nothing, and seizing him by the arm, begins with the strength of the possessed to tear him limb from limb, the other joining in. Finally Agave, picking up his head, impales it on her wand and prepares to return to Thebes in triumph. What a symbol! When reason seeks to deny the power of the unconscious it ends up like this—a bodiless head impaled on the wand, on the ruthless power of nature. Pentheus is finally destroyed by his own mother, or, rather, by the great mother who has swallowed Agave's humanity.

In Agave, too, we are now shown the personal *enantiodromia*. As Pentheus, through his furious hatred of the feminine, becomes a counterfeit woman, so Agave, through her rejection of all discrimination of the masculine principle of disciplined consciousness, becomes a counterfeit man. For she returns to Thebes boasting of her prowess in the hunt, believing that she, a woman, has performed the great masculine feat of killing a lion. Blind to the features of her son (the real masculinity in her psyche), she proclaims that she carries the lion's head on her wand. The tenderness of motherhood has become pride in surpassing the man in his own sphere, a phenomenon with which we are all too familiar. She speaks to Cadmus, her father, "I have left my shuttle at the loom; I raised my sight to higher things, to hunting animals with my bare hands. You see? Here in my hands I hold the quarry of my chase, a trophy for our house. Take it, Father, take it! Glory in my skill!" (p. 413) Here again is the inevitably exact and terrible retribution for Cadmus' sin, when he urged a pretense of worshipping the god in order to bring glory to his own family. His words echo in our minds. "The fiction is a noble

one, for Semele will seem to be the mother of a god and this confers no small distinction on our family." He has it now, this distinction, not through a fiction but through the grisly fact—a trophy for his house. So it is if we dare to treat as fiction the mighty
powers in the unconscious, for consciousness is born only when
we accept these powers but refuse to identify with them.

It is at this peak of horror that the redemption by human
compassion comes, and it is Cadmus who brings it about. He
rises now to the full stature of his age and experience. The false
greatness of his family pride is swept away, and he speaks out of
the true greatness of his spirit. He does not evade, he does not
condemn; no anger, no self-justification mar his words. He does
not deny his legitimate love of his great house, his pride in the
boy who was his heir, nor does he minimize his grief at the humiliation, but it is upon his memories of the boy as a human
being that he dwells with tenderness and love. "This is a grief so
great it knows no size. . . . " To his daughter he says, "How terribly I pity you and then myself. Justly, too, too justly has lord
Bromios, this god of our own blood, destroyed us all." Later, to
the pitiful dismembered corpse: "My son, dearest to me of all
men—for, even dead, I count you still the man I love the
most—never again will your hand touch my chin; no more,
child, will you hug me and call me 'Grandfather' "(p. 418).

However, Cadmus resists another temptation. Pity for his
daughter makes him wish that Agave's madness may last until
death, so horrible the awakening will be. "But if with luck your
present madness lasts until you die, you will seem to have, not
having, happiness" (p. 414). His next words show, however, that
he is done with fictions. Facts, however terrible, will be faced by
him in the future in full consciousness, and he speaks to Agave
with the clear intention of leading her back to reality from her
falsely happy delusion; he bids her raise her eyes to heaven—the
symbol of light, of clarity, of consciousness—and now in a scene
of consummate power, he questions her with gentle skill, leading
her step by step inexorably to the truth, evading nothing for
himself or for her. Yet the stark words are as infused with com-

passion as they are free of the maudlin pity that seeks to cover up the truth.

There are breaks here in the text. Arrowsmith has reconstructed from fragments the speech of Agave, who, aware now of the horrible thing she has done, speaks her grief and her repentance. She too, like Cadmus, faces the truth with dignity and courage, without trace of morbid remorse. She gathers the broken pieces of her life, as we too may gather the broken pieces of our lives, mourning over each one, yet accepting and respecting them and ourselves, so that they may live again, transformed into larger consciousness.

Now into this noble scene of suffering and compassion comes the god himself and speaks the doom of those who have despised him. Utterly without pity, concerned only with retribution, he condemns them all to exile, to constant wandering and worse, and it is borne in upon us with glaring clarity that when the divine image is stripped of all humanity it becomes nothing but the inexorable so-called justice of necessity—the justice without mercy that is the antithesis of the true justice of love. Listen to the exchange in part. Dionysus, in a long speech of bitter condemnation, pronounces sentence on Cadmus and his daughters, harping again and again on the way he has been blasphemed.

CADMUS: We implore you Dionysus. We have done wrong.
DIONYSUS: Too late. When there was time you did not know me.
CADMUS: We have learned. But your sentence is too harsh.
DIONYSUS: I am a god. I was blasphemed by you—long ago my father Zeus ordained these things.
AGAVE: It is fated, Father. We must go.
DIONYSUS: Why the delay? For go you must. . . .
AGAVE: O Father, to be banished, to live without you!
CADMUS: Poor child like a white swan warding its weak old father. . . .
AGAVE: I pity you, Father.
CADMUS: And I pity you, my child, and I grieve for your poor sisters. I pity them.

AGAVE: Terribly has Dionysus brought disaster down upon this house.

DIONYSUS: I was terribly blasphemed, my name dishonoured in Thebes. (pp. 421–22)

What a despicable figure he cuts, this god without pity, with his almost peevish insistence on his wrongs. Agave and Cadmus, rich in their poverty and grief, are most surely now the carriers of the true divinity. Dionysus' interruption is blown away by the wind of their spirit. They ignore him.

AGAVE: Farewell, Father.

CADMUS: Farewell to you, unhappy child. Farewell, you shall find your faring hard. (p. 423)

[No matter how hard the journey, the beautiful human blessing on the wayfarer stands: "Fare you well."]

The same theme is in this play as in the story of Job's greatness when crushed by the pitiless machinations of Jehovah and Satan. As the beauty and dignity of human compassion and conscious suffering, which emanate from Cadmus and Agave, are confronted with the cold brutality of Dionysus' words, there may come to us a new and deeper awareness of the transcendent meaning of the Christian vision of the Incarnation. God became man in time in the person of Christ, but God the Son is an eternal truth. "When Adam fell, God fell into the womb of his mother," said the Lady Julian of Norwich.

Dionysus was a mythological dying and rising god-man. The human unconscious continually throws up this fundamental image; although the god-men of ancient myth tended to be alternately either man or god. They were not wholly god and wholly man in one person. They foreshadowed the eternal truth that redemption and immortality are born only from the sacrificial death of the god-man, but Osiris, for example, was tricked to his death by Set, his dark brother, and Dionysus was dismembered as a child by the Titans. In other words, the pattern was still unconscious. Christ, however, went consciously to his death, wholly subject to the necessity of his fate, yet wholly free, transcending it through the divinity of human compassion, in which the opposites are reconciled, and which is surely the meaning of "dying for the sins of the world."

In this play the god appears in the form of a man, but he escapes from all threats to his person by miracles—he never *becomes* man, and at the end he is shown stripped of all human characteristics—a blind force of retribution. The myth of his death and dismemberment is lived out by an acutal man, by Pentheus, in total unconsciousness, but, even so, his tragedy redeems both his mother and grandfather—and even the chorus is jerked out of its hymns of triumph into pity and humanity.

This is no remote story to move us briefly and forget. It is something that happens in all our lives. Every time we seek to escape some aspect of the human condition, reject the wild forces of the blood or the loneliness of the spirit, project the blame for our own blindness onto another, onto the loved and the hated, onto parent or child, or onto society: each time we *demand* a miracle, escape into daydreaming (that travesty of imagination) or talk about our "rights": then inevitably something both human and divine within us will be dismembered, torn to pieces by the blasphemed God. The answer does not lie in some remote and complicated achievement. It speaks to us in Cadmus' simple words, "I pity you. Fare you well." Catching ourselves again and again playing god in the subhuman or superhuman realms, we can turn in an instant to this redemption if we will but allow the human heart to speak—a thing that is infinitely simple, yet demands a *conscious* sacrifice unto death.

Dionysus, as he appears here at the end, speaks only the cruel logic of the opposites. Pentheus has been wholly destroyed by this logic, but Cadmus, redeemed from his egotistical lip service, emerges an individual man, *related to* the opposites, both subject to fate and free. Repentance does not mean that the consequences of our acts are avoided; on the contrary, it means that they are fully accepted. Cadmus goes forth to long years of pay-ing the price of his blindness, but that he will transcend his fate we have no doubt. Indeed, the god predicts it. It is Cadmus in the true compassion of his humanity who lifts the veil for an instant so that we may glimpse the possibility of finding the Christ within. And so it is that we arrive "God knows where—which is to say, where it matters."

The Little Prince,
by Antoine de Saint-Exupéry

Two famous books have been written in the twentieth century about the "eternal boy," as different from each other as they can be, except in their essential theme of the boy who refuses to grow up. James Barrie's *Peter Pan*, written in 1902, is an entrancing fairy-tale play for children, a fantasy of pirates, fairies, Indians, a loving mother, adventurous children who learn to fly, and the hero boy who can face death as "a great adventure" but who will not live in the human adult world. *The Little Prince*, by Antoine de Saint-Exupéry,[1] written almost forty years later, is not really addressed to children at all, in spite of the words of the dedication, but is a book about the child in adults, an infinitely sad story of the sterility of the world and the lost wisdom and beauty of childhood. It is the tragedy of those people of our times, of whom Saint-Exupéry was one, whose eyes are open to the inner world of dream and image, who know the child's wisdom of innocence and folly, and the emptiness of collective values, but who fail to bridge the gap between their inner vision and the harshness of outer reality. These people are split apart to the

---

[1] Antoine de Saint-Exupéry, *The Little Prince*, trans. Katherine Woods (New York: Harcourt, Brace and World, 1943).

point of suicide, sometimes actual physical suicide, conscious or unconscious, but certainly to the suicide of one value or the other.

From the beginning it is plain that the book is not concerned with the experience of an actual child. A little boy is not separated from humanity in this way, living in a remote and empty place with three volcanoes, one extinct, and sadly watching the beauty of the sunsets. Already the feeling of the tragic end is there. Childhood is sunrise, not sunset, whether we speak of the human child or of the archetypal child in the unconscious of an adult. The child who appears in our dreams speaks of new beginnings, or hints at the wholeness of the end, when sun and moon shine together. Compare the atmosphere of the Little Prince's planet with the Never-Never Land of Peter Pan and the lost boys. (If anyone knows Peter Pan only through Walt Disney's cartoon, let him banish that travesty of the story from his mind.) The Never-Never Land is also remote from the everyday world but vigorously alive with the sparkling fantasy of the child. The boys fly in the air, they live underground, they fight the evil pirates among whom, delightfully, is the "lovable" Smee, they have Indians and fairies for friends, they vanquish wolves, and Peter is rescued from the rising water of the blue lagoon by a bird. When Wendy comes among them the boys turn her at once into a mother, and through her they are finally brought back into the real world, and all, except Peter himself, accept the necessity of growing up, of meeting the dreary world of school and work and responsibility. There is sadness, for most will lose, one knows, their contact with the bright world of childhood and its wisdom, but only so can there be any hope of final wholeness. In Peter there is a hint of the archetype—living in the trees alone but visited each year by Wendy. It is all in light vein, with tinges of sentimentality, but nevertheless we may see in Wendy a hint of the function of the *anima*, connecting the conscious with the unconscious world of fantasy.

It is interesting to compare with this the symbol of the feminine in *The Little Prince*. In the human boy it is the love and care of the mother that connects him (if she is a true mother) with the world and pushes him out of the nest when the right time comes. The *arrested* child in a man may be awakened from his disconnected state by the dawning of an uneasy perception that all is not well with his own feeling life, however "beautiful," and so he is driven to attempt to connect with the world of men. The Little Prince's single rose (his potential relatedness) shows herself as very vain and not altogether truthful, so the boy rejects her and starts on the journey that leads to the earth.

His first experiences are not encouraging. He comes to several other tiny, isolated planets, on each of which a man as lonely as himself lives in his private world, pursuing his empty goal of power or wealth or knowledge or pleasure. On the last one he meets the lamplighter, with whom he feels some kinship—the ordinary man, not imprisoned by an obsession with his own importance, but nevertheless still alone, bound by his daily task and never looking beyond it, lighting and extinguishing his lamp with the setting and rising of the sun every few minutes on his tiny, tiny world, with no time for rest, no eyes for beauty. In his first glimpses of mankind the Little Prince has seen only the polar opposite of the simplicity of the child—that is, the obsession with goals.

The Little Prince now finally reaches the earth itself. He is still alone is the desert, but being on earth he is confronted immediately with the life of instinct. He comes upon the snake, the most earthbound of all, the furthest from human consciousness, who warns him that the world of men and women will prove just as lonely as his planet and reminds him that the bite of the snake can bring death and release. He will not bite the child now for snakes do not harm the completely innocent; only when the Little Prince wishes to return to his planet and comes back to this place will the snake bite him and so release him from the earth. There is an undertone of the cynicism of the devil in this. The snake has no belief in the success of the child's attempt to meet the grown-up world. At the very outset the Little Prince assures himself of a line of retreat from his venture. How unchildlike! He is fatally uncommitted, one feels. He has an insurance policy.

Now the Little Prince crosses the desert looking for men and grows more and more unhappy, until he comes one day to a garden of roses. For the first time he knows that *his* rose on *his* planet is not unique in the universe, and he lies down and cries. His rose for the moment becomes a "nothing but"—that well-known state of mind, the polar opposite of possessive pride. It is at this moment of breakdown that he meets the fox.

Now the fox is a kind of Mercurius or Hermes symbol in the inner world. He is cunning and wise, the trickster and the guide—an image carrying, even today, the numinous intuition of the tie between hunter and hunted. *The Running Foxes,* by Joyce Stranger, is a very beautiful and true story on this theme. It seems proven that an old fox will even invite the hunt to pursue him. It is this animal, the ruthless hunter, the constantly hunted, who teaches the Little Prince what it means to have a friend and what the real nature of uniqueness is.

The fox asks the Prince to *tame* him, and in answer to the boy's questioning he says that to tame and be tamed means "to establish ties"—in other words, to have relationship and responsibility. He teaches the Little Prince that to be unique does not consist of possessing the only rose in all the world—uniqueness comes when love is awakened between oneself and another, be the other fox or rose or person. It is, as we all know, an immensely powerful delusion of the ego, this identification of our personal worthiness with the possession of some special ability or virtue or achievement. The fox reveals the profound paradox that each person's uniqueness is born solely through his or her capacity to "establish ties," conscious ties between self and "other" (whether that other be an outer or an inner reality), and through a willingness to sacrifice the unconscious ties of possession.

The fox now instructs the Little Prince how to tame another. He tells him that with infinite patience he must sit near to him without words and move a little closer every day. It is also good to observe "the proper rites," which, he explains, means in always coming at the same time every day, thus infusing the simple act with the power of ritual—a very sound piece of advice, particularly when it is a question of "taming" our inner images.

Now the fox comes to the heart of his message—the strange paradox that an essential element in the establishing of a tie is the acceptance of parting—even of final parting. The uniqueness of the tie is not lost; indeed, it finds its greatest fulfillment in the inevitable separation, for out of the pain of this experience accepted (accepted daily, not only in the moments of outer loss), meaning is born where before there was no meaning. The gold of the wheat fields, hitherto unnoticed and meaningless to the fox, are now forever alive with beauty because of the gold of his friend's hair. Every wheat field is now unique because of the uniqueness of the Little Prince. The mark of a love that is purged of possessiveness and has become a tie between two who consent to be *separate* is that it does not exclude (so that everything outside it becomes merged in a dreary mass). On the contrary, it begets an intuition of the uniqueness and meaning of every person, every experience we encounter. All of this does not mean that the grief of parting is any less. "I shall cry," said the fox.

The fox's last message is this: "What is essential is invisible to the eye.... It is the time you have *wasted* for your rose that makes the rose so important.... You become responsible, forever, for what you have tamed" (p. 87). That the Little Prince, deeply as he has understood the fox's lesson, has still missed the essential point becomes clear at once. Here is the passage that reveals this misunderstanding, which was indeed that of Saint-Exupéry himself. He is looking at the bed of hundreds of roses and he says:

> You are not at all like my rose. As yet you are nothing. No one has tamed you, and you have tamed no one. You are like my fox when I first knew him. He was only a fox like a hundred thousand other foxes. But I have made him my friend, and now he is unique in all the world.
>
> You are beautiful, but you are empty. One could not die for you. To be sure, an ordinary passerby would think

that my rose looked just like you—the rose that belongs to me. But in herself alone she is more important than all the hundreds of you other roses: because it is she that I have watered; because it is she that I have put under the glass globe; because it is she that I have sheltered behind the screen; because it is for her that I have killed the caterpillars (except the two or three that we saved to become butterflies); because it is she that I have listened to, when she grumbled, or boasted, or even sometimes when she said nothing. Because she is *my* rose. (pp. 86–87)

It is true, but it is not the whole truth. He realizes his responsibility for the rose he has tamed on his planet, accepts its imperfections, and begins to know love. But he does not see that, just as his responsibility to the fox involved accepting his own and the fox's sadness when the moment of parting came, so his responsibility to this rose meant also the acceptance of parting so that the beauty of the rose could live *in* the world, not only on his private planet. So he looks at the hundred roses not with the joy of recognizing the image of the beloved in each one of them, as the fox looked at the wheat fields, but with an almost contemptuous pity. He passes on now to meet the world of men— sees crowds going aimlessly to and fro in trains, talks to a merchant who has invented pills to quench thirst in order to save people from wasting time looking for water. (How very apt an image of our predicament today!) One could imagine that at this point the little fox might have said, "Look beyond what the eye sees and the ear hears and see the human being behind that false mask and take the trouble to tame him. The red glow of his cheeks, even the red paint on the railway engine, could remind you of your rose and give these people and things beauty and meaning. It is thus that you must carry the responsibility to your rose." But the Little Prince misses the point, misses his chance—he thinks only of the beauty of *his* rose, her need of him, and so he makes the final refusal to involve himself in life on this earth, and in clinging to his rose he most tragically betrays her. He starts on his regressive journey to the snake who

will give him death—not the death that is acceptance of life and
of fate, but the death which is refusal of life and of responsibility. Jung has said that the "threat of the snake" points to the
danger of newly acquired consciousness being swallowed again
by the instinctive psyche. This is precisely what happens to the
Little Prince.

Before the final tragedy he meets the airman mending his
crashed plane and asks him for a sheep to take back with him to
his planet. The drawings the airman makes are rejected. The
sheep is too old, or too sickly; finally the drawing of a box is accepted, in which the sheep lies unseen and can be imagined by
the Little Prince in any form he pleases. This would be a delight
in a little boy, but not in a man identified with the child. Surely
it is again a dangerous misunderstanding of the fox's words,
"What is essential is not visible to the eye," which certainly does
not mean that you may turn a real sheep into a private image of
what you would like it to be, but that behind the outer appear-
ances of the sheep, be it sickly or old, there is an essential
uniqueness that may be found if you will "tame" it. This is the
fatal misunderstanding of the infantile personality, whereby the
imagination, the intuition of ultimate truths, may be used to dis-
tort present reality instead of to fill it with meaning.

The man, led by the boy, finds a well in the desert. They do
not just imagine it—they know that the water of life is there
under the arid surface, for the beauty of the desert lies in the fact
of the well. Here the man learns deep wisdom from the eternal
child, but, instead of taking that wisdom to the meeting and
taming of life itself, he will not risk it among men and thinks to
preserve it remote and alone in the sky, so that he must spend his
life with his eyes on the stars and in a continual torment as to
whether or not it still lives. For the Little Prince had taken
something back with him from the earth—the sheep that may
eat the rose. The man had forgotten to add a strap to the muzzle
he had drawn to control the sheep; the unconscious had seen to
that, for we cannot ever ensure the safety of anything. The child,
by coming to earth, had experienced the opposites; he could not

return unscathed to his infantile paradise. He wanted to preserve only that which he wished from his journey, but willy-nilly he took with him that unconscious instinctual urge that could eat the weeds on his planet but could equally well devour his rose and leave him more horribly alone than before. So the man who has refused to hear the *whole* message of the fox, and who tries to preserve the beauty of his inner life isolated from and untarnished by the world, must live with a gnawing doubt forever in his heart. Has the sheep destroyed the rose? It is a doubt that haunts us all whenever we turn even briefly from the fox's message.

So the book ends with the same image with which it began. The actual child's drawing of the boa constrictor with the elephant inside it is full of imagination and promise that the dull adult cannot see, but the image has passed through the separation of the opposites to the opportunity of consciousness, only to end in a regression in which one opposite may be swallowed again in the belly of the other—the tender uniqueness of the rose devoured by the sheeplike collectivity from which the Little Prince sought to fly. The man lives now with his eyes on the stars, seeing their beauty and filled with an insatiable longing, for he has known and loved the child within. But the earth under his feet he has rejected with contempt, and wholeness must forever elude him in this life. It is a moving and beautifully told story with the impact of a tragic truth, but a feeling of sadness and hopelessness pervades the whole book.

So it was in the life of Saint-Exupéry himself—a man of potential genius who never broke his identification with the eternal child. Someone who knew him well wrote of him that he had in equal degree "real and profound mysticism, great appetite for pleasures of the senses and total irresponsibility in daily life." Also it was said that he was "an extremist in all things. He could not bear contradiction." These are the marks of this identification. It is interesting that some psychologists have said that a large proportion of airmen are of this kind, particularly, perhaps, the dare-devil pilots—fighter pilots of the war, test pilots.

Saint-Exupéry was rarely happy except when flying. It was an essential need of his nature—almost as though he were constantly trying to reach his Little Prince, alone and sad on his planet. In the air he felt free of all the deadening smallness and meanness of the ordinary man, of whom he writes with such withering contempt. Even his greatest admirers admit this contemptuous attitude in him. He was a pilot of great skill but caused everyone the greatest anxiety by what was known as his "absent-mindedness." He would forget to let down his undercarriage; lost in his inner dream, he would fly off course and suddenly return to reality to find himself in danger, and so on. There is an unconscious courting of death in such men—a yearning for the bite of the snake that can restore them to the lost child. Finally he did meet death in the air, living out the symbol. His plane was lost over France on the last mission permitted to him in the war. No trace of it was ever found. It just disappeared as the Little Prince's body had disappeared.

He had been, as usual in the case of such personalities, his mother's special favorite, and he adored her all his life. Barrie, too, had this devotion to his mother. In *Peter Pan* the father, Mr. Darling, is shown as stupid, even pettily cruel. Saint-Exupéry's marriage was a stormy, irresponsible affair, as one would expect, of violent quarrels, separations, and equally passionate reconciliations. When separated from his wife he would write movingly of his responsibility for his "poor Consuelo." He genuinely felt it but he could not live it. He could never live responsibly because he had rejected one-half of the fox's wisdom, and so his delicate perception of real values remained "in the air," constantly threatened by the "sheep." The sheep, double-sided like all archetypal images, is the symbol of both innocence and of the collective stupidity that he so bitterly despised. The images of his unconscious—the King, the Wise Man, the Practical Worker, the Lover of Play, the Servant—remained forever on their lonely planets, possessive and meaningless to the end. For the child, who could have brought all of them to earth, if he had heeded the message of the fox, had chosen to return to his planet. Thus the man could not grow to that true meeting of opposites in which the inner child remains vividly alive but "tamed," related to outer reality. Saint-Exupéry had genius, and he did *not* evade his responsibility to express it. But inevitably his genius did not mature. Perhaps only in *The Little Prince* did it truly come to earth, for in it he describes his own tragedy with power and truth. Many have acclaimed *The Wisdom of the Sands* as his greatest book. He thought so himself. Beautiful as so many of the sayings in it are, it remains somehow remote from humanity and therefore tinged with unreality and sentimentality. In it the king of a desert kingdom speaks all his thoughts about life and its meaning. It is significant that near the beginning of the book the king goes up onto a high tower and *looking down* on men he pities them and resolves to heal them. He then claims to have "embellished the soul of my people." The king is concerned with "people," not individuals. He is alone with his rose to the end. The book's French title is *La Citadelle*—the tower, the fortress, the safe place from which the king looks down on the world.

One such boy-man came for analysis many years ago. His quickness of understanding, his intuitive awareness of the unconscious and eager enthusiasm were full of promise. But he was not seventeen; he was near thirty and had no notion of what it meant to accept the responsibility of manhood. Such men often have very great charm, carrying as they do the image of the eternal promise of youth. Older women will forgive them again and again their enormities! This man was continually in and out of jobs, and it was his wife, older than himself, who earned their basic living. As with Saint-Exupéry, partings and reconciliations succeeded each other with bewildering speed. He was not a flier but courted death through reckless driving of cars. When his license was revoked it never occurred to him to stop driving— that risk just made it a bigger thrill! The taking of wild risks in the outer world is a compensation for the inner refusal to risk the infantile psyche in a meeting with the responsibilities of a man. He made endless good resolutions, with complete sincerity, but they broke down at the touch of reality and the necessity for discipline. Yet how much he knew of a wisdom closed to the dull and respectable! He died violently in an accident. He had returned to his snake, refused to leave his infantile paradise and expose his rose to this world.

The *puer aeternus* personality is rarely met in such extreme form. But for every one of us there is a warning in the images of Saint-Exupéry's story. We need to become conscious of the partial ways in which we identify with and so banish to a lonely planet our inner child. For whatever we identify with is lost to us as a reality. If we will hold to the child's value of innocence and folly while at the same time fully accepting the realities of space and time; if we will endure the separations through which possessiveness and the demand to be "special" are dissolved; then our feet will be firmly planted on the earth while we watch the stars in their courses. Only then, having emerged from the easy paradise of unconscious childishness, we may "tame" and "be tamed" by the Child within, who brings true uniqueness and ultimate wholeness. This lovely image comes to us in our dreams, grave and gay, wise and innocent, the promise of the beginning and the fullness of the end. "Unless ye become as little children [become as, not identify with] ye shall not enter the Kingdom of Heaven" (Matt. 18:3).

We turn now to some words of Jung: "The child is the beginning and the end. . . . The child symbolises the pre–conscious and the post–conscious nature of man—his wholeness. . . . The child is all that is abandoned and exposed and at the same time divinely powerful; the insignificant, dubious beginning and the triumphant end. The 'eternal child' in man is an indescribable experience—an imponderable that determines the ultimate worth or worthlessness of a personality."[2]

---

[2] C. G. Jung and C. Kerenyi, *Essays on a Science of Mythology* (New York: Harper Torchbooks, 1963), p. 96.

The Story of Saul

Saul's life had all the elements of great tragedy. He was a man broken by his fate, a noble failure, who disobeyed the divine vocation laid upon him and thereafter was utterly rejected by Yahweh until his death. Yet Saul emerges with a kind of greatness and power to move us that David, with all his heroic qualities, cannot surpass. His story has particular relevance in these days when so many are broken by the same kind of possession by the unconscious that overthrew Saul.

Rivkah Schärf, in her paper "King Saul and the Spirit of God" (Guild of Pastoral Psychology), has pointed out the essential differences in the accounts of the two elections to kinship—Saul's and David's. Whereas David was anointed "in the midst of his brethren" and the Spirit of the Lord immediately came upon him in direct association with his vocation as king, Saul was anointed in secret by Samuel, who told him that he had now been chosen as king but that the Spirit of the Lord would not come upon him until later, when he would meet a band of prophets on the way and would receive the spirit of prophecy. In other words, the "spirit" was not directly connected with his outer task as king, but was a gift to his inner life.

The word "prophecy" has come to mean a foretelling of the future, but in those days a prophet was a person capable of ecstasy, of being filled with the spirit. The prophet was the "seer," or, as we would now say, one in whom the deep unconscious has been activated and to whom is given the choice between meeting and relating to the powers thus released or succumbing to possession by them. In the former case a true "prophet" or seer is born—a person burning with the strength and beauty of an inner vision, a channel for the wisdom of God, but one who nevertheless remains human, related to this gift of the spirit and never identified with it. But, one who allows ecstasy to remain on the emotional level, who loses his or her ordinary humanity or is incapable of the kind of obedience that the inner voice demands, will be split and destroyed by this "gift of the spirit" and will end up in the clutches of the demonic side of it, as did Saul.

It seems that Yahweh made an abortive attempt in Saul. Israel had hitherto had no king. It had been a theocracy, and Yahweh was angry that the people now demanded a king; he even accused them of idolatry. Nevertheless, he saw that a king was a necessity if his people were to survive in the struggle with the heathen, so he told Samuel to give in and anoint a king. There seems to be considerable ambivalence in God's attitude at this point (ambivalence in the God-image of Israel). Yahweh's choice of Saul was perhaps an attempt to resolve that ambivalence by anointing a man to be king who had also the capacity for ecstatic inner vision. Saul was therefore called to be a great military leader, a ruler of power and great possessions. At the same time, however, he was called to be a man of the spirit, following the inner way, which has always involved for the seer separation from the world, from outer possessions and power. It was an almost impossible demand, and Saul was split in half and destroyed by it. Yahweh appears to have been trying to bring to birth over night, so to speak, the totality—a union of opposites in one man who would be both king and prophet in Israel. We could say that the soul of Israel was trying to have its cake and eat it too—that is, to become a strong, rich nation in this world and at the same time to retain its peculiar spiritual vocation as God's chosen people. It is indeed a conflict that emerges in every individual soul, but Israel attempted in Saul an impossible collective solution, and the personal Saul was broken by his fate. Perhaps that is why a later legend speaks of the people's "debt" to Saul.

It is said that God "repented" of his choice. Next time he knew that he could not ask so much of his kings, just as he had never asked so much of his prophets. David was given the blessing as king, not as prophet, and in the light of this it makes sense that, although his sins were much more frequent and seemingly more serious than Saul's, nevertheless he was never deserted by the Spirit of God, never rejected. To Saul God had given his greatest inner gift, and therefore one disobedience at a vital point could wreck the whole. It was as though the failure of Saul made it finally clear that no man could carry this double burden and that kingship could only be reconciled with prophecy in the inner world of the individual. Therefore it was of peculiar significance that Jesus was born of the royal line of David—that the Messiah is also the King, but that his kingdom is "not of this world." This was the rock on which the Jews stumbled when Christ made his claim. They still could not conceive of a king who had no outer power and was not a great leader of his people in the world. They had not learned the lesson of Saul. The Priest–King remains in legend, but only in legend (Prester John), expressing an inner truth.

There are three separate accounts of the election of Saul. The first account is of his secret anointing, followed by his first experience of the Spirit when he met the prophets. When Samuel tells him of his destiny, Saul is already frightened of it— "Wherefore speakest thou so to me?" (1 Sam. 9:21) The second account tells how Samuel called the people together to cast lots and the lot fell upon Saul. The story tells how Saul, knowing his weakness, had hidden himself as though wishing still to evade his fate. Even after this he seems to have gone quietly home, and some of the people still did not accept him, until the city of Jabesh-Gilead was besieged and sent out a cry for help. Then the Spirit of Yahweh came again to Saul in the form of anger against the heathen and great courage, and he rose up and entered into his kingly task and freed the city. Then the people fully acclaimed their king.

There followed a series of wars against the heathen. Then came a command from Yahweh through Samuel, and Saul was told to go out and destroy the Amalekites and not to spare any one of the people nor any part of their possessions or flocks. Saul now showed that he had allowed power and wealth to weaken disastrously his obedience to the inner voice. Victorious, he spared both Agag, the enemy king, and all the best flocks, though he slew the citizens and the poor flocks and told Samuel he had fulfilled the will of God. We might be tempted to ascribe to Saul the motives of a noble rebellion against this barbarous demand for slaughter, but this would be an anachronism. For the primitive, possessions were a part of the owner's personality and the meaning of Yahweh's command was simply that no part of the evil attached to the "heathen" should be allowed to survive.

Saul's motive in sparing the flocks was plainly that he could not bear to give up such riches. The temptation of power was too strong for him; he had begun to covet possessions. Worst of all, when Samuel rebuked him, Saul made excuses. Had he admitted his fault and repented, the sequel might indeed have been different, but instead he justified himself by a lie. "The people spared the best of the sheep and of the oxen to sacrifice unto the Lord" (1 Sam. 15:15). He blames others and invents a noble motive for the disobedience. Then comes the terrible retribution. "And Samuel said, 'Hath the Lord as great delight in burnt offerings and sacrifices as in obeying the voice of the Lord? Behold to obey is better than sacrifice and to hearken than the fat of rams. For rebellion is as the sin of witchcraft. . . . Because thou hast rejected the word of the Lord he hath also rejected thee from being King" (1 Sam. 15:22–23). One feels that Samuel is speaking here as one seer to another. For the man who can inwardly hear the voice of God the primary sin is disobedience to that voice and the inevitable result is "witchcraft." The Spirit remains but turns demonic. For the ordinary man's disobedience there would be retribution, but not that kind.

Saul admits his sin, but immediately makes another excuse. He says he is afraid of the people. This again is an impossible excuse in the seer, though forgivable in another. Then, as Samuel turns to leave him forever, Saul catches hold of his robe and it tears in his hand—the symbol surely of the split that now begins in Saul—the separation from his brother prophet, Samuel, the part of himself that has been truly given to God. Thus, Saul shows again, in his grief at the now inevitable loss, how far his corruption has already gone. He begs Samuel to delay his going in order to maintain his, Saul's, prestige before the people. He is full of remorse, but will not pay the price of humiliation and repentance. He has chosen worldly power and betrayed the inner voice. The great love between Saul and Samuel comes through these few verses with the force of tragedy: "And Samuel came no more to see Saul until the day of his death: nevertheless Samuel mourned for Saul" (1 Sam. 15:35). God himself, as it were, admits that he has asked too much of the man he chose: "The Lord repented that he had made Saul king over Israel" (1 Sam. 15:11).

From now on the disintegration of Saul proceeds. "The Spirit of the Lord departed from Saul and an evil spirit from the Lord troubled him" (1 Sam. 16:14). Notice that the Spirit was still "from the Lord." This shocks our modern rationality, but in truth it was the same spirit as before though now it had become an emotional state of possession. The gift of the Spirit is a *capacity* for vision. It can carry us to wholeness if we accept the price, or it can consume and destroy our humanity. The story of Saul makes utterly clear the turning point. If we *use* this capacity to acquire any kind of power, prestige, or personal possession, however seemingly harmless or even "good" our superficial motives may be, then we open ourselves to possession by the dark side of this power. This is the theme of Tolkien's *The Lord of the Rings* from beginning to end. This is why Saul's tragedy can make so great an impact in this age of reaction from nineteenth century materialism, when we are surrounded by attempts to reconnect with the numinous in so many forms—drugs, astrology, tongue-speaking, depth psychology. We yearn for the gift of the *Ruah*

Yahweh, the Spirit of God, and we are thereby exposed to the dangers of Saul in extreme form, because for the most part we seek the experience without the commitment, and so confuse the end with the means. To refuse the kind of obedience that is the price of vision is to abrogate our humanity, and then indeed, as Samuel said, "Rebellion is as the sin of witchcraft." A breakthrough of "vision" is very frequently followed by dreams that insist on the importance of the ordinary day-to-day human values and disciplines, so great is our danger of floating off into some kind of inflation, or "mission," or spiritual possessiveness, whereby we fall prey to witchcraft in the unconscious, as Samuel predicted for Saul.

In our moments of choice how do we *know* that we are obeying the voice of truth? We can only do our best to discriminate our motives, free ourselves from conventional opinions, watch our dreams, use our intelligence, together with our intuition, weigh the values involved and the effects on other people, and then act wholeheartedly from the deepest level we know. If our choice proves to be a mistake, it will be a creative mistake—a mistake leading to consciousness. If it is a question of a big change in our lives, something almost always comes from without to meet the urge from within, and we have a chance to *recognize* our way—either by resisting a temptation or by accepting a new attitude. If our commitment to our "fate," to the will of God, includes the willingness to pay the full price, we will not go astray—we will relate to the Spirit within, not succumb to possession by it. There is no rule to tell us whether this or that is the right attitude, the right way to behave in all circumstances.

Recurrent fits of melancholia now fell upon the king. David appeared at court, having slain his giant, and Saul surely recognized, unconsciously, in the newly anointed one his own refused vocation, and inevitably in his split condition he both loved and hated him. Already, however, we sense the nobility and the enduring love in Saul, which no failure or disaster can ultimately tarnish. It is this that accounts for David's lifelong devotion to him. Perhaps at this point if Saul had stood up and fought his "evil spirit," he would have been saved from the evil to come, but he seeks only soothing music, a panacea, from David, the symbol of new life, new opportunity. He clings more and more frantically to his old attitude toward power until, when he hears the people exalting David's achievements above his own, he succumbs to his envy and fear, and hatred turns to murder. He is sucked into the abyss and kills, or tries to kill, all those whom he most loves. He attacks David with the javelin, then drives him from court (unconsciously intending, we may feel, to save him for the future). Later he throws the javelin at his own beloved son, Jonathan. The horrible crime of the murder of the priests of Nob, who have innocently helped David in his flight, is the measure of his blind and bitter rejection of his own call to holiness. Saul the tender-hearted, Saul the seer, has come to this.

Only for one moment after David leaves does the veil lift, and we see that the old Saul lives. After David has spared his life, when Saul lies asleep and at his mercy, the two speak across the gulf—the space between their armies—and Saul says: "Is this thy voice, my son David?" And Saul lifted up his voice and wept. And he said to David: "Thou art more righteous than I; for thou hast rewarded me good, whereas I have rewarded thee evil. And thou hast shewed this day how that thou hast dealt well with me . . . wherefore the Lord reward thee good for that thou hast done unto me this day. And now behold I know well that thou shalt surely be king and that the kingdom of Israel shalt be established in thy hand" (1 Sam. 24:17–20). Saul's true heart is not dead, only submerged. As always with us all, chance after chance is offered. Had he stripped himself then and there and gone into the wilderness, the final horror would have been avoided. Jonathan, his son, his flesh and blood, might have survived to stand beside David the king, with his gentleness and his wisdom. But Saul is not capable of *action*, though his heart's generosity still lives, and this is what lifts the story to the level of high tragedy.

The end comes with the final betrayal of the seer within. All sense of contact with God is gone. Saul is rudderless, unable even to decide when to fight the Philistines and when to refrain, and he descends finally to seeking guidance from the ghost of Samuel, his dead inner wisdom, through a witch—he, the king who forbade all practice of witchcraft in the kingdom when he was strong in spirit. Samuel's prophecy about witchcraft is fulfilled. The witch of Endor raises Samuel's ghost, but the dead thing can promise only death: "Tomorrow thou and thy sons shall be with me." So Saul, finally accepting his fate, goes out to fight and his three sons with him, and, after he is wounded, he falls on his sword and his three sons are killed with him, as though there can be nothing left behind of his failure.

Nothing is left—and yet the immediate sequel to his death begins to establish the *meaning,* the strange, dark beauty in this story of unendurable conflict and defeat. The men of Jabesh Gilead, who have felt personal love and devotion to Saul all through the years since his rescue of their city, rise up and, at great risk to themselves, go and cut down his body from the walls of the Philistine city where it hangs dishonored and take it home with them to give it honorable burial. It has been said that a man can only be judged by his effect on others, and we become aware as we read that the dominant reaction to Saul of almost everyone with whom he came into close contact was one of love. Samuel loved him, David loved him, Jonathan loved him; one senses the loyalty and love of Abner, the captain of his host, of his servants and his soldiers, watching him in his dark moods and bearing with him; even the witch of Endor shows him a kind of maternal tenderness after his encounter with Samuel's ghost. Only a man who is himself full of love can inspire this kind of devotion. Saul betrayed or murdered or tried to murder everyone he loved best, but it is clear that the darkening of his consciousness, the surrender to demonic possession, or to the destructive split in his personality, as we should say, could not finally extinguish the validity of his real love, the nobility of his essential nature. So we have a tragedy, with all its cathartic power, instead of a meaningless story of a diseased mind and a jealous tyrant. David's lamentation over Saul and Jonathan sweeps away the cruelty and the failure and lifts the image of Saul into beauty: "Saul and Jonathan were lovely and pleasant in their lives and in their death they were not divided; they were swifter than eagles, they were stronger than lions. Ye daughters of Israel weep over Saul. . . . How are the mighty fallen!" (2 Sam. 1:23)

Finally a Jewish legend pays the highest tribute of all to the memory of Saul—God himself gives proof of his love and ultimate acceptance of his servant. The legend tells that there was famine in Israel, and David, the king, sought to find the reason for God's anger. Finally God spoke to him and said that it was because of Saul—because due honor had not been given to him since his death. So David sent to Jabesh-Gilead and Saul's body was dug up and found to be uncorrupt, and David ordered that the coffin should be carried into every part of Israel, to every village, so that the people might pay homage to the body. So it was done and Saul was buried in his home: "And when the Lord saw that the people had paid due honor to their king, he became compassionate and sent rain upon the land" (2 Sam. 21:14).

A record of facts and deeds tells one kind of truth about a great man, but a legend tells truth of another kind, in another dimension, projecting us for a moment beyond the opposites to an intuitive vision of the whole.

Frodo's Mithril Coat in *The Lord of the Rings,* by J. R. R. Tolkien

I n *The Lord of the Rings* Bilbo gave to Frodo a mithril coat that the dwarves had forged in the depths of the earth. This coat was very light and very strong and was worn by Frodo underneath his clothing, so that even his companions did not know about it.

There are two questions I want to ask about this coat: Why was the coat given to Frodo at that particular point on his journey? Against what kind of danger did it protect him?

During the first part of his journey, as far as Rivendell, Frodo was carrying the Ring more or less unconsciously. He left home because of Gandalf's urging, without understanding very much about it or having any notion of where he was going. He trusted Gandalf's wisdom, he greatly feared the Black Riders, and only knew he must keep moving on. He was extremely vulnerable at this time and was indeed wounded almost to death before he reached Rivendell. After the council of Elrond, however, he was clearly aware of the task before him, of the goal of his journey, and of the stupendous dangers of the way ahead. He had been asked to make a fully conscious choice. He, a little man who had lived the most unheroic kind of life in his comfortable home, was now to carry this great responsibility, to undertake a journey that from every reasonable point of view was bound to fail, and to face unknown dangers, supernatural as well as natural. He was asked if, instead of running from the black power, he would go open-eyed into the heart of the darkness. He made his choice. He said "yes" to his destiny, not out of any heroic feeling of specialness, not because he felt brave and strong and worthy, but in full knowledge of his weakness and fear, simply because he had been asked to do so by his friends, whom he trusted and loved. It was at this moment of his complete acceptance of exposure to every kind of danger, without thought of success or failure, that he was given the protection of the mithril coat.

This coat would protect Frodo against all the lesser dangers—against the unseen thrust in the back, the chance arrow, the spears and darts of orcs and other servants of the Dark Lord. It would *not* protect him from the greater dangers. From these his only protection lay in secrecy. They could not be fought face to face.

It is not difficult to see the relevance of these things to ourselves. It is surely true that in the life of every person there is one major turning point—a moment of choice when one's basic will (the Frodo in oneself) may say "yes" or "no" to the challenge of one's own individual way and to the inevitable suffering and danger it involves. It is certain that, if we say "yes" in this moment, then, in proportion to the single-mindedness of this decision, we too are given protection against lesser evils, against the consequences of mistakes due to ignorance or weakness, against the attacks of those who do not understand, and against invasions from the mass unconscious. There is an image of this choice in T. S. Eliot's play *The Family Reunion.* When Harry makes his great decision and all lesser aims are stripped from him, it is then said of him that he is entirely safe from ordinary human risks such as accidents, etc.

The same law is seen at work in all the lesser choices that must maintain and reaffirm the first "yes" throughout our lives. Once started on the journey, we can never let up. Every day there is the temptation to go back on our choice, fall back into the unconscious, but each time we decide to take up a responsibility we have sought to evade (having hitherto persuaded ourselves, perhaps, that we are not worthy, or that it is not "fair," or that the particular burden is too heavy for us, and so on), then, in the very moment of our willing self-exposure and conscious acceptance of the task, no matter what the consequences, we can often literally feel a new invulnerability to the poisoned darts of our own false guilts or resentments, of our blind projections or false humility. And poisoned darts these things certainly are, invading us and clouding our thought and feeling, so that relationship becomes impossible, and our deeper goal is lost sight of in the fog. It is a great paradox. Strip off our outer protective clothing, the careful muffling of our previous self-esteem or personal comfort, and immediately the strong, light mithril coat is there, underneath our clothing and unseen by the world. Often we must tear down concrete walls that we have built to defend ourselves against reality. If only we could realize that the thicker these walls are, the more vulnerable we become!

There is a type of dream with which we are all probably familiar in some form. The dreamer is chased by an enemy, and if the dreamer will only turn and face it, or freely open the door, the threatening figure is seen as no danger at all. The enemy is transformed, perhaps, into someone in need of help, or someone with a vital message. "What if, in turning to meet the enemy, we find him more dangerous instead of less so?" In that case we had better run away again, if we can, or, if not, accept the seemingly hopeless fight. Both actions are seen often on Frodo's journey. For example, Frodo and Sam ran from Shelob, but when finally caught, Sam fought her and won against seemingly impossible odds. Notice that the mithril coat could not save Frodo from the great evil of Shelob. Only the light of Galadriel could help him here. The only vital thing is the willingness to face the danger and to see it consciously, no matter what it is. It is then that safety may come at the very brink of disaster.

It is important to know to "run away" in the right sense, or rather how to hide oneself, especially for those exposed in their work either to constant contact with collective mass attitudes or to the unconscious of other individuals. Nurses, doctors, and psychologists belong in the latter category, and for them it is of the first importance to be constantly aware of where their responsibility begins and ends. It is just as great an evasion of reality to assume responsibility in places or on levels where it does *not* belong to us as to refuse our true responsibility. For women, especially, the temptation is very great to allow emotional involvement to drain them of energy, so that they have no strength left for the true, objective task. The emotion may be there and strongly felt, but it must be contained, hidden, so that it cannot blind and exhaust us. A possessive kind of emotion is just as great an evasion as any other frightened rejection of clear-cut, objective responsibility and love. It is this same kind of thing that exposes us to invasion from the unconscious of those close to us in personal relationships. Whether the emotional reaction is of fear, love, hate, or even curiosity, it will so cloud our vision that there is no more possibility of a true I-Thou relationship, and mutual invasion is the outcome. The only cure is in constant awareness and discrimination of values and in the acceptance of "pure fact," which is love in the true sense. Then indeed we each have a mithril coat.

To return to those working in the world, in constant contact with the collective attitudes of society, there are two kinds of protection. One is the same as that outlined above—wholehearted acceptance of each particular job or responsibility taken and the containing of emotional reactions—and the other is, I believe, a conscious effort to ensure that on leaving office or shop one re-establishes contact with the individual way. A *rite de sortie* is needed. If possible, some contact with another who is on the same journey is a very great help—or perhaps fifteen minutes spent in active imagination or in consciously doing nothing. Each one can discover his or her own technique for shedding the tentacles of mass thinking.

There is another question we may ask. Why was Bilbo the giver of the coat? Bilbo was Frodo's uncle-father, the representative of the "ancestors" who pass on to us the heritage of the past. At the moment of a man's acceptance of his own unique way, this heritage becomes consciously his. His connection with his parents and ancestors is no longer an unconscious force pushing him this way or that, hindering his recognition of his own personality, but becomes for him a true support and protection, as he accepts both the dark and light aspects of this inheritance. When a woman dares to be true to herself as distinct from her parents, her nation, her race, she is immediately able to relate to, and therefore draw strength from, the values of her personal and impersonal past and the powers of the deep unconscious, whether negative or positive. She is no longer blindly possessed by them, and so she is in an altogether new way protected—protected by the mithril coat forged link by link, experience by experience in the depth of the unconscious, and passed on to her personally by one like Bilbo who has lived his own life to the full. I have heard dreams in which a great value was found, for example, in the basement of the parents' house, but such a dream will come only after a long and painful struggle to be free of the parents' superficial values and attitudes.

Finally, there is much to be learned from Sam's invulnerability in the story. He is the only one of the hobbits who goes entirely unscathed through the whole journey, and he wears no mithril coat. He has no need of it, for he has that very rare thing, a simple, natural innocence against which all attacks fall harmlessly to the ground. He is completely single-minded, wholehearted, in all his acts. He loves his master and cheerfully follows him without question, no matter where he leads. Like all men, however, he too has his moment of vital decision. Most aptly it seems he must choose between Bill, the pony, and his master—between the completely instinctive innocence, perhaps, and human single-heartedness. There is only one moment after that when he is threatened by conflict, by a split in his devotion, and this comes to him during the brief time that he carries the Ring. He wants for a moment to keep it from Frodo. (For such as he the Ring of power would be a very great danger. The very wholeness of his devotion would mean that he would go over wholly to the Dark Lord.)

In these days there are very few indeed to whom it is given to travel this way of simplicity, of natural, unsplit innocence, but Sam's wholeness gives us a prevision of that ultimate innocence to which a person may come eventually in full consciousness, if he or she will carry the Ring to the very end, as Frodo did. Meanwhile, we can recognize in the smallest things that whenever we are completely wholehearted in our action or feeling, without ulterior motive or conditional response, then for that instant, however brief, we are invulnerable, set free from all the insidious dangers that threaten the soul from outside or from within.

"The King and the Corpse"*

This is an Indian story about a king, a good and generous man, who sat daily in his audience chamber hearing petitions. Every day for ten years a beggar-ascetic would come into the hall and offer him a fruit, then go away without a word. The king thought this an odd but trifling matter and would simply pass the fruit to his treasurer, who each time tossed it through a window into a treasure house without opening the door, and took no further notice. Then one day a tame monkey escaped from the women's apartments and got into the hall. The king handed the fruit to the monkey instead of to the treasurer, whereupon the animal bit into it, and out dropped a shining jewel. At this, the king, astonished, asked where the other fruits were, and they hastened to the treasure house where, amidst all the rotting fruit, lay a pile of precious jewels. The next day when the beggar-ascetic came, the king asked for an explanation, and the beggar claimed his reward. He told the king he wished him to undertake a hero's part and help him with a magic enterprise, to which the king consented. He was told to come on the night of the new moon,

* Heinrich Zimmer, *The King and the Corpse* (New York: Pantheon Books, 1956). I wish to express gratitude to the late Dr. Zimmer for his book of tales from all over the world and his interpretation of the title story, "The King and the Corpse." I am indebted to him not only for the story itself but for some of the seed thoughts in my essay.

alone, to the burial ground of the city, where the dead were cremated and criminals hanged. The beggar-ascetic's name was "Rich-in-Patience."

The king gave all the jewels away, and on the appointed night, in spite of his horror at the eerie noises of spectres and demons, met the beggar-ascetic among the funeral pyres and found him drawing a magic circle on the ground. The beggar told him that his task was to go to the far edge of the burial ground, cut down the corpse of a hanged man, and bring it back to him. The king obeyed. He found the corpse hanging, cut it down, and was about to pick it up when the corpse laughed. The king, realizing that a ghost was in it, spoke to it, whereupon the corpse immediately flew back into the tree. Again the king cut it down, this time silently, and lifted it onto his shoulders. Then the ghost spoke to him and said that he would while away the journey with a tale. The tale concerned the abduction of a young girl, which finally brought death to the girl's old parents, and the ghost ordered the king to judge which of the characters was to be held guilty of the deaths, telling him that if he could come to any conclusion about it he *must* speak it out, otherwise his head would explode into one hundred pieces. The king knew that if he spoke the corpse would immediately fly back to the tree, but he had no choice; and so it came about. Back the king went, cut down the corpse again and started off. Again the ghost told a tale and demanded a judgment, and again the ghost and corpse flew back to the tree when the king had spoken. Twenty-four tales were told in this way, and twenty-four times the king gave a judgment, the corpse returned to the tree, and the king doggedly went back and started again.

Then came the twenty-fifth tale. In this story a widower and his son wanted to marry a widowed queen and her daughter. But owing to a misconceived oath, the father was compelled to marry the daughter and the son the widowed mother. Each couple had a son, and the ghost demanded that the king define in a precise term the relationship between those two children. The king, striding along with his corpse burden, was unable to do this. The paradoxical relationship was both this and that; the children were uncle and nephew, nephew and uncle through both mother and father. The king's human judgment was silent.

Now, the ghost spoke again, telling the king that he had passed the test and could have the corpse. He revealed that the beggar-ascetic was in fact a wicked magician in disguise who was plotting the king's destruction. The guileless king was to be tricked into worshipping the corpse, which the beggar would set up as an idol, forcing the ghost by spells to stay in it. The king would be told to bow his head to the ground and the magician would then strike it off with the king's own sword and offer him as a sacrifice to the corpse. Thus he would gain power over the spirit world. The ghost told the king there was only one way of escape—to meet guile with guile. He must ask the magician to demonstrate to him the correct way of prostrating himself and then quickly cut off the magician's head, whereupon all the power of the magician would pass into the king himself in glorious and positive form. Thus it came to pass. The king with a slash decapitated the sorcerer, and then cut out his heart and offered head and heart to the spectre in the corpse. Then there was great rejoicing. The spectre was set free, all the ghosts and dead souls were released from fear of the sorcerer's spells and Shiva himself appeared in glory and thanked the king for freeing the powers of the spirit from the evil ascetic. So the king again took up his human life, no longer the old superficial, guileless youth, ruling his people benevolently but without understanding, but a wise and courageous ruler who knew himself and was beloved of god and man.

Who is the beggar-ascetic, "Rich-in-Patience," who comes every day to the king with his seemingly worthless but actually very valuable gifts? He is the polar opposite of the King's conscious personality. The king who is rich, both materially and in capacities of mind and heart, who need deny himself nothing, carries in the unconscious, as do we all, the beggar who has nothing that the world esteems—an unrecognized part of himself that seems to have no importance whatever in his life of ease and sincere good work. He is a good king, working hard each day to render justice to his people, generous and brave, guileless and well intentioned. Yet every day there comes to him this beggar, not to beg, but to offer him a hidden gift, a hidden jewel of great price. But the king does not eat the beggar's fruit. To him the gift is trivial and, though he may have wondered at first over the oddity of this daily persistence, it is plain that through the years it has become so familiar a daily occurrence that he hardly even notices anymore. We may imagine that gradually he has become more and more identified with his persona—his role in the world. Success and ease have made him complacent and have imperceptibly increased his blindness to the inner world. So may each of us slip into unawareness; yet day after day a "fruit" is offered from the unconscious. Perhaps it is some seemingly trivial reaction to an experience that does not fit in with our concept of what we are or should be, and we discard the unwelcome impulse or thought as irrelevant. Or it may be a recurring dream or image, quite meaningless, we think, or a persistent fear, or an often repeated kind of external experience that we dismiss with the phrase "Just my luck!" If these things damage our image of ourselves, we never stop to bite into them, to find their core, never realize that the despised beggar shadow is trying over and over again to wake us up to the hidden value of that which we despise. Rightly he is "rich in patience."

The beggar himself does not remain unaffected by our constant neglect. At the end of the story we realize that the rejected beggar has accumulated in himself in negative form all the energy that the conscious personality refused, so that he has acquired "magical" powers. An unconscious content pushed further and further down becomes more and more autonomous, and its power over us grows more deadly the less it is recognized. It becomes a spell over us, which cannot be broken except by a conscious descent into the place of ghosts and demons. The king's increasing identification with his outer power turned his beggar shadow into a destructive power complex, operating autonomously and "plotting" his ruin. It is a perfect image of the double nature of the archetypes. They constantly offer a new value, a new opportunity for awakening; yet at each refusal they steal energy from consciousness, until one day we are shocked into facing their ambiguity and may, if we will, undertake the journey downward that leads beyond the opposites.

The manner of the king's awakening is full of meaning. A monkey escapes from the women's quarters! The segregated territory of the animal, his emotional nature, has never been allowed to impinge on his careful and logical giving of masculine judgments in the council chamber. We may assume that it has not been a matter of conscious discipline, but of compartmental living. Sooner or later, in the person who lives in this rational one-sided, manner, the monkey—a spontaneous, instinctive impulse—will break in and disrupt for a moment the solemn conscious proceedings. The king does not drive the monkey away, and this is the great turning point. He is saved by his sense of humor perhaps—a very frequent savior. He laughingly throws the beggar's fruit to the monkey, showing in this one action both his contempt for the beggar's gift, yet perhaps also his half–conscious knowledge that only the instincts can wake him up. The monkey immediately bites into the fruit and the jewel tumbles out. So we one day may carelessly and merrily follow some impulse, thinking it a small matter, and then perhaps suddenly glimpse the enormous value of that other side of ourselves that we have long despised.

It is vital that at this point we recognize that our light-hearted discovery is a very serious matter. We cannot just sit back and enjoy the accumulated treasure. It is said in the story that the king did not covet material riches and immediately gave the jewels away. Once awakened, and because all through his period of one-sided conscious effort he has been sincere and doing his best, he immediately knows that the jewels themselves are not important and that the value they stand for must now be earned. He must pay the price for the beggar's gifts. He asks the beggar what his desire is.

The self-centered, insincere person, on discovering his repressed other side, may simply give him or herself over to it, relinquishing conscious values. Thus, he may end up in worse shape than before. For instance, a puritanical person will suddenly be overwhelmed by his or her repressed sensuality and, instead of coming to terms with the unlived shadow, will identify with it. The sensualist turned puritan is in a like case, though the world may applaud the spectacular "conversion." One repression is simply exchanged for another, and there is no growth. The despised value must be accepted *without* relinquishing the truth in the previous attitude, and the way to this redemption, this union of conscious and unconscious, involves for many, as it did for the king, a journey into the dark place of ghosts and demons, where the long search for self-knowledge begins.

So the king willingly descends into the place of the dead. The beggar, in this double role, has offered the king his chance of redemption, which is bound up with the threat of destruction. He is sent to fetch the corpse of the criminal and finds in that dead body a ghost. This ghost is surely the king's own inner vision, banished from consciousness through the years of careless ease, imprisoned in the corpse of that which symbolizes the furthest conceivable opposite of kingship—the condemned and executed criminal. Maybe the king himself in this council chamber had condemned this man to death—justly, no doubt, according to the laws, but without love or understanding, without recognition of the essential coinherence of each human being with all others, of king and criminal, rich and poor, good and bad.

The corpse, however, is unburied. It seems that the symbol of "killing" in the unconscious (except sacrificial killing) is usually an indication of deep repression, but the symbol of "burial" means that there is a possibility of transformation, of conscious assimilation of the "dead" value. The immense importance of burial rites to all primitives conveys this inner truth. If a body remained above the ground, the spirit of the dead would haunt the living. In our language, a repressed complex will possess the psyche from the unconscious, and it is precisely like a haunting by an unseen ghost. But a burial rite is a conscious act—a returning of the body to the nourishing earth, a letting go of the spirit to the Creator. The inner meaning of the dead value is now released and available to consciousness. The legacy of the "ancestors," of past experience, or of the good or bad outgrown attitudes is now our own.

The criminal in the king cannot yet be buried. The weight of the dark, unknown corpse must be long and patiently carried before the moment of transformation when ghost becomes spirit and the corpse is united with fertile earth.

The king's test involves precisely the acceptance of the beggar-shadow's qualities. He is stripped of his power and wealth, must submit himself like a beggar to the whim of the ghost, must find the discipline of the ascetic, and above all, must be "rich-in-patience," doggedly refusing to lose heart or give up in the face of repeated failure. The twenty-four tales, the judgments, each one revealing more of himself, and yet involving, as he knows, a return to the beginning again, seem to bring him no nearer to accomplishing his task of taking the corpse to the beggar's magic circle, where the transformation could take place.

It is significant that the king decides that the guilt for the tragedy told in the first story lies not with any of those immediately involved, but with the *king* of the country who, by his lack of awareness and responsibility, has allowed such things to go on behind his back. It is a clear acceptance at the outset of his own true guilt and blindness—an acceptance without which no inner journey is possible. To us it means the refusal to blame others, our parents, our luck, our fate, and the taking up of full responsibility as human beings for our situation.

What is the meaning of the threat that he *must* answer if he can, or his skull will explode, and of the fact that as soon as he does answer, he must go back to the beginning and cover the old ground again? To refuse to answer, to fail through fear of consequences, to refuse to stand by the best human judgment we can produce in any given situation, is to deny the whole meaning of what it is to be human, for the skull is the container of consciousness, and if we are not prepared to be true to our present stage of awareness, then there is no possibility whatever of our growing to the next. All of us know this process. As soon as we have won through to clarity and decisive action in some situation, conflict, or state of emotional turmoil, a new confusion arises, and we feel that we are back at the beginning again. In fact, it truly is as though by daring to take responsibility for a clear decision or attitude we *invite* return to the beginning again. If only (we think) we hadn't been so definite, this new problem would not have arisen. No, but our head would have split into one hundred pieces—a familiar sensation, surely! Thoughts and feelings flying in every direction, the will confused, no coherence or sense of meaning anywhere—this is the inevitable result of the refusal of *choice*. If we are silent, the ghost also is silent, and we go on walking unconsciously into the magician's trap.

The point of the twenty-four judgments that must be given with full integrity is that we cannot jump to that which is beyond the right or wrong of human ethics and values, to the place where the opposites are seen in their wholeness. We cannot evade the hard daily work of using every faculty of mind and heart to arrive at our own individual point of view, while never confusing this with universal truth. The king's answers are the fruit of his individual effort to discriminate values, but are in no way a final resolution of the questions posed. There are many other possible answers.

Throughout this weary journeying back and forth, the king is surrounded by the eerie shapes and weird cries of the demons who inhabit this dark place. How easy it would have been for him to be distracted by fear, or curiosity, or even by the noble feeling that he must be a hero, attack these demons, and destroy them, as befitted a king! So are we often lured away from the carrying of our corpse, by nameless fears, by irrelevant "missions," or by many other kinds of distraction. The king took no notice at all, concentrating his whole attention on the immediate task, that of listening to the inner voice and answering the questions it posed, and so finally, when it must have seemed to him that this repetitive journey would go on forever, comes the question that has no answer in human terms.

The children in the twenty-fifth tale are both this and that. No amount of thought or depth of feeling can produce an answer, a definition of their relationship. The story is simply a hint that every concept contains the opposite of itself, that all human judgments must ultimately prove one-sided, falling short of the truth. It has the feeling of a Zen *koan*, which, by asking an unanswerable question, will perhaps at last shock a person into the jump beyond the categories of human reason, beyond cause and effect, to the glimpse of ultimate reality called in Zen *satori*. At the beginning of his journey, the twenty-fifth tale would likewise have reduced the king to silence, but it would have been the silence of frustration and blindness, not the inner silence of dawning vision. Therefore the ghost does not ask the twenty-fifth question until all the previous work is done.

Now the king is ready for the face-to-face meeting with the beggar magician, for the dangerous moment when the sacrifice will be made one way or the other. He may succumb to the greed for power—the last and greatest temptation of the person who has won through to individual freedom and greatness of spirit. In this case his humanity will disappear, offered up as victim to the corpse and the ghost by the possessive demon that uses spiritual power for the purposes of the ego. Or he will cut out the head and heart of his inner magician, sacrifice all the greed of the ego, and so liberate the powers of the spirit and the simple values of the earth, that they may unite at the new center of his life.

It is another of the last-ditch moments that recur in every myth. All our efforts and choices in little things cannot save us from these moments, but because of long devotion in these things, we are able to hear the "ghost" when it opens our eyes to the wiles of the magician. The guileless king would have refused to hear this warning at the beginning of the journey. He would have been an easy prey, for it is very difficult to see through the disguises of the will to power, to distinguish between "black magic" and the miracle of real sacrifice and transformation. But now the king's eyes are open. He is no longer tricked by the magician's fine ascetic exterior, and so at the crucial moment it is the latter who is blind and who puts his head down, to his own undoing.

The god Shiva, in whom creation and destruction are reconciled, now appears, and the king's vision includes for a moment the totality of heaven and earth. He returns to his kingdom, to the same task as before, and we may imagine the pain of this return. Jung has described it, after telling of his great vision of the Marriage of Heaven and Earth. Nothing has changed to the outward eye; the king rules and gives judgment as before. Yet everything has changed, for he lives from a new center of wisdom and wholeness.

The Symbolism
of Water in the Bible

The Bible begins and ends with images of water. "And the earth was without form and void; and darkness was upon the face of the deep. And the Spirit of God moved upon the face of the waters" (Gen. 1:2).

"And the Spirit and the Bride say come and let him that heareth say come. And let him that is athirst come. And whosoever will, let him take the water of life freely" (Rev. 22:17). This is the last verse (except for the brief epilogue) of the Book of Revelation. From the formless beginnings to the ultimate vision of the Holy Marriage there is no life without water.

Everyone knows that all living cells began in the oceans—that water is the great mother of all life, and that the long journey to consciousness began in the depths, but no scientific language can explain the "why" of the first dawn of consciousness. For this we must turn to the language of myth and symbol. In Genesis, as in many other myths of origin, it is the movement of the Spirit of God which begins the creation. Something enters into the womb of the waters, and there is life. It is as though God first differentiated all the opposites, which existed in their totality within himself, by making a division between them. It then followed that there could be no new life on any level of being without a coming together of these opposites in an act of creation.

The pairs of opposites now multiply. Light is born, and "God divided the light from the darkness." Then comes yet another division. Having created the firmament of heaven, "God divided the waters which were under the firmament from the waters which were above the firmament" (Gen. 1:7), and then proceeded to bring the dry land, which he called Earth, out of those waters that were *under* the firmament of heaven. It is perhaps a hint at the outset that the symbol of water stands not only for the unconscious origin of all life rising from the lowest depths but also for the highest conscious vision—the "living water" of which Christ spoke, the "water of life" with which the Bible ends. Thus we may finally realize that "the above is as the below," the end is the beginning, and life is a circle, not a straight line.

It has been said that this myth is simply a primitive explanation of the origins of rain from above, but this in no way invalidates the symbolic truth of the images in the realm of the psyche. The scientific truth that the coming down of rain and the condensing upward of ground water is a circular process, is an image of the inner truth. We have advanced very far indeed along the way to the scientific understanding of the physical universe, but we have allowed this one-sided development to obscure and devalue the understanding of the truths of the psyche, so that now we must return to learn from the intuitive wisdom of the so-called primitive.

The myth now tells of the growth upward of all life on earth. The up and the down must be thoroughly differentiated and experienced as separate before we can discover that the waters above the firmament are as the waters below, and at every stage of the way there are, throughout the Bible, stories in which the symbolic meaning of water is emphasized. Materially we cannot live without water; spiritually and intellectually we shrivel up and die without the water of the unconscious, which is both above us and below us, and it is a characteristic of our age to imagine that we can invoke the fire and air of the spirit and the intellect while ignoring and devaluing the water and the earth, the passive, nourishing feminine values, the wisdom and mystery of the depths. Water without fire drowns us; fire without water burns us to ashes.

Let us consider three of the great biblical stories about water: Noah and the flood, Jonah and the whale, and the baptism of Jesus. The flood theme occurs in mythologies all over the world and certainly refers to some great worldwide catastrophe. It is nonetheless inwardly significant. There are times in the lives of most people when the waters rise and threaten to overwhelm all their hard-won achievements. The flood occurs in the myths at a time when humankind has advanced some way beyond its earliest beginnings; God has become angry at the total misunderstanding of the purpose of his creation, and decides to wipe out in one act all their puny self-centered achievements so that he may make a new start through Noah, the one just man who has remembered God.

This kind of new chance is offered, perhaps once in their lives, to all those individuals who have become entangled in false values, in the pursuit of possessions, success, or power in any form, and have yet within them a "Noah"—a small, unregarded part of themselves that could become aware of the futility and emptiness of these goals and values. It comes often at this stage as an outer catastrophe—financial disaster, serious illness, loss of a loved person, and so on. It may seem as though all meaning has disappeared from living; the mainspring has broken. Now there is nothing to be done but build an ark for the small core of faith—faith in that which is greater than personal catastrophe—and let the Noah in ourselves ride the waves of misery and despair, until at last they begin slowly to recede. Then dry land appears, and, with all the past swept clean, we may begin again to build. The instincts, too, will be in the ark; they do not die, for our "Noah" could not live if he were cut off from their simple strength.

The story of Jonah and the whale also concerns those moments when the waters swallow us, but in a very different way. It is no longer a question of taking refuge in an ark from the rising water, but of deliberately *choosing* to plunge into the dark ocean. We may, indeed, be spared the flood if we are able to make this conscious choice. Jonah has been running away from the voice of God; he has been disobedient to his individual truth, just as humankind was disobedient before the flood. The result for Jonah was the threat of the "flood," not only for himself but for all his companions on the ship. Then comes his moment of decision. He will willingly pay the price and save his companions. The sailors, seeking the guilty one in order to throw him overboard, restore calm by a repression of the "shadow," by the projection of their personal guilt, and for many people this may be the only possible way. But for Jonah it is the crucial choice in which he accepts responsibility for his own darkness, and so he saves others as well as himself. He goes to meet the deep unconscious, willing to die if necessary, and he is swallowed by the great mother fish, the whale. He finds an "ark," in the depths of the sea this time, which is also womb, and from this (after the symbolic three days and nights) he is reborn, emerging again on dry land to a new life of free obedience to the voice of God.

This is the biblical version of the night sea journey that occurs in myths all over the world and at every stage of the development of human awareness, appearing as often in the imagery of people's dreams today as in the ancient stories. Anyone who seeks to emerge from infantile attitudes and achieve individual maturity must pass this way, must go down willingly by one road or another to meet the darkness of the whale's belly, and so discover that this womb of the great mother may in due time give birth to a new personality. All too often it is assumed that the second birth will come through a continual striving upward, through ignoring the water and calling only on the fire from heaven. To be born again of the Spirit there must still be a womb. It is not a question of ascension, but of birth. Spirit and water must meet as they did in the beginning before God can say, "Let there be light."

The night sea journey comes generally, to those who con-

sciously go to meet it, only once as a major transforming experience, but over and over again we must repeat the going down in
some form or other, for every ascent requires an equivalent descent. There is no straight line to the heavens, and it is when the
fire burns in the water that we come to vision. In one version of
the myth, the sailors light a fire in the whale's belly—a beautiful
symbol of the necessity of bringing the light of consciousness and
the warmth of the heart to each confrontation with the darkness
of the unconscious.

In the far more evolved New Testament story of the same reality, the return to the water is no longer described, as in primitive myth, in terms of a literal, external happening, but as a
symbol of the inner life of the individual. (For the primitive the
exterior and the interior are not separate realities, but one.) St.
John the Baptist preached the way of repentance and renewal
and introduced the symbolic rite of immersion in water to en-
force his meaning. His emphasis, however, was wholly on the
purification, the cleansing power of water, until the baptism of
Jesus revealed the whole mystery. When Jesus descended into
the water, the Holy Spirit came down upon him; water and fire
were one in a moment of revelation, and he was seen as Son of
God as well as Son of Man.

The rite of baptism in the Church preserved this symbolism. It
is not immersion in the water alone that redeems. Still less is it
the simple washing away of sin, but the meeting of fire and
water, conscious and unconscious, spirit and matter, God and
man. The water of the font is blessed on Easter Saturday by the
lowering of a lighted candle three times into the font, and by the
breathing of the priest three times over the water. A child is
born a "son of man," of nature only, and the practice of infant
baptism is the immediate recognition of the potential unique individual wholeness of every human being, of one's destiny as a
"son of God" as well as a "son of man." To this one may come in
due time when he or she is ready to *return* to the water of the
beginnings in full consciousness, and so be born again "of the
Spirit."

There are other, lesser stories in the Bible that carry the same basic meaning—the healing and transforming power of the maternal waters of the unconscious. We may take three instances. In the Old Testament there is the story of Naaman, the rich and powerful Syrian who was a leper, and who came to the prophet Elisha to be healed. He was told to dip himself in the River Jordan. He was outraged by such a humiliating request, but when he consented to do this "little thing" he was cleansed. It seems such a "little thing," not worthy of effort, when we are asked, for instance, to attend in analysis to some image from the unconscious, to draw a picture like a child, and so on, and our proud and rational attitudes violently resist such a proceeding. We seek some spectacular way to healing. We think that simply descending into the water won't do. Yet this simple *consent* is the bringing of the light of consciousness into contact with the dark water.

In the New Testament, Christ himself sends the blind man to wash in the pool of Siloam after he has anointed his eyes with spittle, water from his own mouth, mixed with the earth. And in the story of the pool of Bethesda we meet again the image of the healing water that is breathed upon by the Spirit and becomes a transforming agent. In this case it is as though Christ emphasizes that the return to the water is an inner, not outer, process. He heals directly the impotent man who is waiting for someone to put him into the water when the "angel," the Spirit, comes down to "trouble" it. The man has been trying for years to get to the water, but has not had enough strength. His effort, his patience, are the important thing, and the healing comes.

In each of these stories the physical disease healed is an apt image of a psychic disturbance. Naaman, the rich man, despising poverty and dirt, was smitten with the uncleanness of leprosy— that which made a man untouchable, set him apart in a negative way as his pride had made him feel himself set apart as superior. His healing comes from submitting to the humble, simple thing. The man blind from birth may symbolize one who, bearing the weight of humankind's collective blindness, had remained for the whole of his life unaware of individual values, wholly dependent on his environment, but who yet, we may guess, has been growing slowly through his courage and integrity and is ready for the meeting with Christ and the sudden breakthrough that a return to the waters may bring. His behavior later, his refusal to lie when threatened by the Pharisees, is a hint of this. The impotent man at the pool is a victim of weakness, and the story promises that even those of us who have not the strength to go down consciously to the waters may reach transformation through constancy and patience in long suffering.

Even more powerful to move us than the stories is the poetry about water in the Bible. The land of Israel, particularly Judea, is dry and arid for three-quarters of the year, and water was in a special way for the Israelites the life-giving symbol. "Then shall the lame man leap as an hart, and the tongue of the dumb shall sing; for in the wilderness shall waters break out, and streams in the desert. And the parched ground shall become a pool, and the thirsty land pools of water" (Isa. 35:6–7). "The desert shall rejoice and blossom as the rose" (Isa. 35:1). As without, so also within. "Blessed is the man that trusteth in the Lord, and whose hope the Lord is. For he shall be as a tree planted by the waters, and that spreadeth out her roots by the river, and shall not see when heat cometh, but her leaf shall be green, and shall not be careful in the time of drought, neither shall cease from yielding fruit" (Jer. 17:7–8). We need have no fear of the times of dryness and emptiness, nor of the withering heat of collective prejudice, if our roots reach deep enough down to the waters under the earth.

Jesus met a woman by Jacob's well in Samaria and asked her to draw him water from the well—the ancient task of the woman. And Jesus said, "Whosoever drinketh of the water that I shall give him shall never thirst; but the water that I shall give him shall be in him a well of water springing up into everlasting life" (John 4:14). The waters of the earth flow always downward, down to the rivers, down to the lakes, down to merge in the immensity of the oceans in which all may drown: all fire on the earth leaps upward, consumes everything it touches, and disappears into the air. Water and fire destroy each other. But when the "living water" springs upward and the fire of the Spirit descends to meet it, then "The Spirit and the Bride say come" and we who are thirsty may drink freely of the water of life.

The Story of Jacob

In the book of Genesis the theme of the two brothers at enmity begins with Cain and Abel, continues with Isaac and Ishmael, and culminates in the much more complicated story of Jacob and Esau. With the Fall and the knowledge of good and evil began the inevitable split between person and person and between ego and shadow within a person. The life of Jacob is a turning point in the Old Testament accounts of this struggle with the dark brother, which every human being must encounter on the long road to the healing of the split.

Abel took the first step towards consciousness by realizing that the offering to God involved the shedding of blood, which in our language would mean that the approach to the divine must involve the death of an old attitude that costs our lifeblood, not just a giving up of something we can well spare. Otherwise Cain would have killed Abel simply out of envy. How often do we remain at the Cain stage, wiping out immediately any glimmering of a new way? The next fraternal conflict was resolved by the banishment of Ishmael, the son of the bondwoman, so that Isaac, the son of the freewoman, might carry the torch of consciousness and civilization forward unmolested by the wild, regressive brother who would resist free growth. In the infancy of consciousness this separation is necessary, but if maturity is to come it must not endure. If the unacceptable, regressive tendencies are thrust completely out of sight, out of mind, they do not therefore cease to exist. Either we hand them on to our wives, our husbands, our children, or our friends, or we are eventually swallowed by them ourselves. We shall see how Isaac both hands on his conflict and suffers it himself in physical blindness.

Jacob and Esau were twins, and according to the legend, they started fighting even before they were born, in the womb of their mother, Rebecca. Esau emerged first, with Jacob close behind, holding onto his heel. From birth Esau was red-skinned and red-haired; in fact, he was hairy all over. Later he was known as Edon, the red one: red is the color so often associated with evil. Set, the brother and enemy of the god Osiris in Egypt, was also the red one, and Mephistopheles by tradition wears red. Red is the color of the impulsive, emotional, instinctive nature, which, if in control, can swallow all civilizing tendencies and so become evil. If, on the other hand, it is repressed and denied, it will leave the conscious personality dry and unreal, and finally more completely at the mercy of its fiery power. The story of Jacob can bring much insight into the way that every person must follow if he or she is to avoid either falling under the domination of the red one or banishing all instinctive wisdom from the conscious personality.

Esau was hairy and red, the cunning hunter, full of rude strength. Jacob was smooth and white-skinned, a man of the "tents," his mother's favorite, cunning of mind but not strong of body, sensitive, fearful even, and, we may imagine, a lover of beauty, hearing already the inner voice to which his brother's ear was closed. Jacob's first recorded act is the trick whereby he persuades Esau to sell his birthright. He knows that his brother is stupid and greedy, unable to resist his immediate desires or to see the relative importance of the different values of life: so he prepares a red pottage and offers it to Esau at a moment when the latter is extremely hungry after a day's hunting. The insistence on "red" hints at the symbolic nature of the story. Esau is offered food that will nourish his already dominant quality, his desirousness, and his hunger for this food is so great that he parts with his birthright in order to satisfy it immediately. For him this meant that he held the right of the firstborn in contempt, the right that brought in those days not only the material, but the spiritual leadership of the tribe. For us our birthright means the high dignity of our free will and capacity for consciousness. Every time we sell out on our essential values, driven by fear or the desire of the moment, we relinquish our freedom, our birthright, and so become the "child of the bondwoman," dominated, for the moment anyway, by the red one within. It is easy to see why Rebecca, the mother, with her sure intuition, knew that Esau must never receive the blessing.

Most people react to the story of Jacob with a bewildered feeling that by our standards it is all wrong. Why does Jacob, who behaves throughout in the most reprehensible manner, tricking and deceiving first his brother, then his father, then his uncle, get all the rewards? To answer this we must look more deeply at the meaning of "the blessing." The birthright involved leadership and power, but the blessing of the old father, given to the chosen son, was much more than this for the people of God. It was the handing on of the light, the spark whereby a man became aware of God's voice, of the divine within himself. Now, as then, it is essentially the same. A true blessing may pass from one person to another insofar as the one who blesses has become a channel for it. (Never, of course, can it be given through the ego, the personal will.) Or it may come collectively through a true ritual. In either case, its effectiveness must depend on the state of receptivity in the recipient.

The father's blessing bestowed on his son was, in those days, a ritual act. As we have said, beyond the outer gift of riches and leadership, it laid on the son a great spiritual responsibility, for Yahweh spoke directly to the bearer of the blessing. In later times the blessing passed from anointed king to anointed king, from prophet to prophet, and the beautiful story of the taking up into heaven of Elijah illustrates the immense care that must be taken not to allow the blessing to fall on the wrong person. Elisha was told that he would receive a double portion of Elijah's spirit *only* if he were present and saw with his own eyes the passing of the old man. Elijah tried to go off alone, and only by constant vigilance (in us, that daily awareness that is so hard) did Elisha succeed in being there with his eyes open when the miracle happened.

We may imagine the possible result had the blessing been given to Esau. As far as outer matters went, Esau was more than competent, indeed far more straightforward and physically brave than his brother; but the blessing, bringing the capacity to "see visions and dream dreams," would surely have brought personal as well as collective disaster. If the "red one" starts dabbling in matters of spirit, he becomes the prey of superstitious and dark imaginings and is soon caught in magical practices. Esau would probably have been running after sorcerers and witches, as Saul did when, having received the blessing, he was disobedient to it. As it was, Esau lived his life in the way that was valid for him. He became just as successful outwardly as Jacob, simply by remaining what he was—a hunter, a crude man, but true to his own nature. The blessing would have ruined him, turned him dark and evil. So with the "red one" in the unconscious. If we feed him the red pottage, his own food, let him be his own earthy self, he will not possess or destroy us. If we deny his nature, try to make him into something spiritual, and so push him out of sight, he will start practicing "magic," and we shall be under his spell, whether we recognize it or not. He must be up where we can see him and meet him, and accept or reject his influence in our lives.

In Jacob's case, we are at first given no clue to his capacity for carrying the blessing—except the hint about his perception of his brother's false values in the pottage incident. He is timid and reluctant when his mother proposes the deception of Isaac. Rebecca is a woman who consciously faces an enormous risk, takes on a great burden of guilt, for the sake of an absolutely vital issue, and so exposes herself to the certainty of losing all she personally holds most dear. The future of the people of God is at stake. She is vividly aware of the necessity that the blessing be carried by Jacob, the sensitive, highly intelligent, intuitive son, rather than by the sensual, earthbound Esau. Of course there must also have been the purely personal desire that her favorite son should have the power—what woman does not feel that?

Nevertheless, we may believe that Rebecca served consciously the greater purpose. "On me be the curse," she says, in the full and lonely acceptance of the guilt that must fall on her because Isaac was blind. For this blindness surely has a symbolic quality. He was blind because he, too, really knew that Esau could not carry the blessing, but he lacked the courage to disinherit him. Perhaps this was, as we hinted earlier, a result of his own complete separation since childhood from his brother, Ishmael. Never having faced his own conflict, Isaac could not now make the hard sacrifice involved in disinheriting his elder son. It is obvious from the story that he could very easily have let himself know that he was being deceived. He persuaded himself to disregard the recognized voice of Jacob. Also he could not have failed to know, when he ate Jacob's meat, that he was eating kid, the meat of the tents, and not venison, the hunter's meat that he had asked Esau to provide. He just lay on his bed and let Rebecca take on all the pain and guilt of deception. It is notable, too, that he made very little fuss afterwards, did not even seem angry, as though he really agreed in his heart.

We come here to the curious but constantly repeated theme that the blessing is bestowed not on the "good," dutiful man but on the sinner—on Jacob, on David, on the prodigal son, on Paul—to name a few. This does not, of course, mean that a sinner who remains possessed by his or her sins can ever carry the blessing, but it does assuredly mean that one must be *able* to break loose from all conventional codes when it is a question of an essential value—provided he is willing to accept the guilt (which remains guilt whatever the motive) and the payment and suffering it involves.

In the story of the prodigal son the sinner is preferred because he has had the courage to break away from the safe family pattern, even though he has for a time succumbed completely to the "red one." The necessary suffering and repentance are experienced before the blessing is given. In the primitive story the blessing comes first, but the long years of payment are implicit in it. Only those are blessed who consciously, or unconsciously at first, have consented to this payment. This is an entirely different thing from the dangerous assumption that the end justifies the means. Those who embrace this attitude are precisely those who refuse the payment. They feel no guilt in the breaking of the law because they complacently delude themselves that their motives excuse them. They are among the cursed to whom Christ referred in his apocryphal saying about the breaking of laws. "If thou knowest what thou art doing, then thou art blest, but if thou knowest not what thou are doing then art thou cursed." It is exceedingly difficult truly to know what one is doing, and for most of us it is a matter of falling through our weakness under the power of the "red one" and waking up afterward.

The question, then, is not whether Jacob was a "good" man and had earned the blessing, but whether he had the capacity to hear the voice of God, and the courage and devotion to risk everything, reputation, safety, even relative goodness, in order to follow in obedience. We shall see that however unattractive we may find Jacob's character, he undoubtedly had this devotion. As it was for Jacob, so it is for ourselves.

So Rebecca and Jacob sinned, the blessing was given and received, and their sin was no less because it was a necessity of the spirit. Now they must pay. Rebecca paid immediately and all her life long in the loss of Jacob, for she never saw him again. This is the typically feminine payment—a willing separation from the beloved son. Jacob paid, as we shall see, in the many experiences of his long life.

The first consequence for Jacob was that he was forced to break away from his mother, to stand on his own feet. Hitherto he had lived under her influence, protected by her and therefore subject to her. The whole scheme for obtaining the blessing had been hers; he had done nothing but reluctantly agree. But though his fear had forced her to say "on me be the curse" (Gen. 27:13), he *had* agreed, and therefore accepted all that must follow. Isaac had uttered no curse, but the inevitable retribution could not be evaded.

Rebecca, knowing that Esau's fury could easily lead to murder, immediately sends Jacob away, hoping it would only be for a time. She knows that Esau's emotions are violent but short-lived and easily forgotten. She persuades herself on the surface, as we so often do, that the price will not be very heavy, though in her heart she must have known otherwise. She invents a polite fiction for Isaac, who could not stand, it seems, even that much truth, and tells him that Jacob must go and seek a wife among her own people (they disapproved of Esau's heathen wives). It was a fiction superficially (since her real reason was Jacob's safety) and yet profoundly true, for a man, having wrested the leadership from his shadow, his regressive other side, must now go on a long journey in search of his *anima* and his true feeling nature.

Jacob sets out alone. For the first time he must act and choose without his mother. One may imagine his loneliness and doubt as he journeyed, wondering, surely, if his deception of his father would invalidate the blessing, if he would be rejected by God. Thus everyone of good will, after a big step to freedom, involving perhaps a great hurt to a much-loved parent or friend, will look back in fear, wondering whether he or she had been merely self-willed to no purpose. Jacob lies down for the night with his head on a stone—as though, perhaps, he would say, "Whatever I have done is hard fact; I will accept, lay my head on this hard reality." Then the heavens open and he sees the angels of God ascending and descending, and God speaks to him. The blessing is confirmed. He sees the going up and the coming down and knows intuitively the constant exchange between earth and heaven. Then, waking, he swears to build one day a house of God upon this spot. This is his acceptance of the responsibility of the blessing, the full commitment of his life to obedience to the voice of God.

He continues his journey with new strength and sureness and comes at last to the well at the entrance to his uncle's village, and to his meeting with Rachel, the love of his life. It is a beautiful image, this meeting with the beloved beside a well. Her first action is to draw water for her love-to-be. So also did Rebecca herself, though it is noteworthy that in the earlier story Isaac did not go himself to find Rebecca; his father Abraham sent a trusted servant to seek her out for his son, and he found her beside the well. Isaac throughout seems entirely contained in the collective pattern and does nothing individually; hence, surely, his blindness later.

Jacob comes to the well and looks upon Rachel as she draws water for the sheep, and he loves her. The woman, the *anima*, is performing her vital function of drawing up the water of the unconscious that the man and his flocks, his instincts, may drink. A man depends always either on the woman outwardly or on his *anima* inwardly to bring him this life-giving water, without which his masculinity is sterile, his intellect dry, and his feeling dominantly emotion. So, in the first opening of his love, Jacob comes to his uncle Laban's house and enters at once on the next phase of his payment for the blessing.

Laban, one feels, was an older, more seemingly civilized version of the crude Esau. Materialistic, cunning, superstitious, he recognizes Jacob's value to him and immediately exploits his nephew's love for Rachel by demanding seven years' work for her. Jacob willingly agrees. Here we notice the difference of character between him and Esau. He will wait and work, subjecting himself consciously to the earthy Laban, and suffer cheerfully for the great value of his true love. His instinctual urge can wait—it demands no "red pottage" on the instant. The seven years pass and he asks for his reward, and now comes almost literal retribution for his earlier deception; the deceiver is deceived in circumstances that are a repetition in reverse of the original event. Whereas before there were two brothers, the red one and the white, now there are two sisters, the red and sensual Leah, the white and sensitive Rachel. The father sends Leah in to Jacob in the dark. Jacob does not recognize her and is bound to her for life. Ironically, Laban's answer to Jacob's reproaches is to point out the unbreakable custom that the elder daughter must be married before the younger. The poetic justice is complete.

Jacob has been altogether too naive. He must have thought, "Now that I have paid my price, I can unite with my beloved and we can go off and be free of this crude 'red thing' forever." This is the mistake into which we all fall at one time or another. After each emergence from a period of darkness and struggle we imagine that *now* we can go forward without the "other," the ugly one. Perhaps Jacob, like Isaac, *could* have known; perhaps he half-consciously recognized the inevitable rightness of this thing. A man cannot without great peril idealize or spiritualize his *anima*; he cannot live only with this aspect of her, or the other side of her will turn evil. Jacob, however, is forced willy-nilly to take both aspects, and so the earthbound Leah becomes the fertile mother to many of his sons.

Rachel, who nourishes his inner vision, must wait long and suffer the agony of seeming sterility before finally she brings to birth the bearer of the blessing, Joseph, the beloved son. Jacob still has a long apprenticeship to serve before he can give life to this son. He is allowed to marry Rachel seven days from the time of his taking Leah, but he is bound to Laban for seven more years of service. Only after the "true son" is born, after, we may say, he has come by long patience and work to the birth of the new possibility of objective vision, which will carry the light into the future beyond his own personal life, is he set free for the next journey.

We are given a vivid picture of Rachel's sufferings during this period, of the jealousy between the two sisters, of her sense of her own unworthiness and the projection of her own resentment even onto her beloved Jacob. How well we know these reactions! She is even driven to send her maid Bilhah to Jacob's bed so that Bilhah may bear a son on Rachel's knees (a recognized custom), and she enters in imagination into the pangs of labor and birth in order to assuage her humiliation at her barrenness. This "make-believe" was not futile. It was all part of her inner preparation for the true birth. Maybe we could compare it to the active imagination we can enter into, which is truly like the labor of childbirth inwardly, when we are up against a terrible rigidity of consciousness.

Jacob has now served his twice seven years. He has fathered new life both on this earth through Leah and in the world of the spirit through Rachel, and it is time for him to return to his own country to take up the mature tasks of later years. First, however, he carries out another "deceit." He persuades Laban to promise him all the spotted and ringstraked goats and sheep in his flocks, including those that shall be born during the year. He then practices some sympathetic magic on the ewes. Every time they conceive he sets up striped stakes for them to look at, and in due course their offspring are spotty! We may think this is a dirty trick, but all modern advertising is based on the same "magic." Show people the name of a product often enough and they will begin automatically to think it the best brand when they go shopping. Jacob was simply a good businessman as well as a visionary! Laban came out the loser because he had no imagination; there was really no actual deceit involved.

With his wives and his sons and his flocks Jacob sets off in secret from Laban's house, for he is afraid that his uncle will hold him by force, and he journeys for three days, not knowing that Rachel has stolen her father's household gods—the little images that protected the homes of those who were ignorant of the one God. This is an interesting episode. It looks on the surface like a somewhat childish, mean trick, but it perhaps symbolizes a deeply significant moment in Rachel's development. It is the moment of her final breaking with her father, and again we meet the motif of theft. All conscious growth is in one sense "stolen" from the point of view of nature and of the unconscious. Prometheus had to steal the fire from heaven. In stealing the household gods Rachel is breaking the *spell* of the father image. It is a theme in modern dreams, this stealing of something that gives power to the spell of the magician, the hitherto all-powerful unconscious conflict. In the story it has precisely this effect, for it cannot be mere chance that *after* the stealing, Laban has a dream in which the true God of Jacob orders him to be friendly to Jacob, to make peace with him no matter how angry he may be. He follows Jacob and, in spite of his resentment about the theft, makes a covenant with him in which they set up a clear boundary line. In Jacob there is now discrimination and conscious acceptance of all that Laban represents. Rachel does not confess or give back the images. She just sits on them while Laban searches, and his spell is broken. It seems that woman is always the one to practice guile!

The journey continues, and the moment approaches when Jacob must again meet his brother Esau. At first he is overcome by his usual timidity; Esau's resentment may still be fierce, he is a man of war who will easily overthrow the peace-loving Jacob. So Jacob takes human precautions and divides his possessions and servants into two bands, hoping to save at least half of them, but it is clear that he knows all this to be superficial. He must meet with his brother as with his own soul, face to face, alone and unarmed. At the brook Jabbok he sends all his company ahead, including Rachel and her son. Alone he will spend the night in wrestling with himself, with his fear, with his inner shadow brother. This time there will be no trick about it; he must find the deeper blessing. "And there wrestled a man with him until the breaking of the day" (Gen. 32:24). There is no overt mention of an angel in the biblical account. Brief but intensely vivid, what an extraordinarily moving account it is of a man's struggle with the unknown in himself! It expresses his absolute determination to know this stranger, to prevail, to find its "name." He realizes that the seeming enemy is the one who can bless him, this time individually and from within, not ritually and from without, as in his early, unconscious days. He is wounded in the thigh, exhausted from long hours of effort and

says, "I will not let thee go except thou bless me" (Gen. 32:26).
So must we all hold on with the last ounce of strength, through
all the ups and downs of our interior struggles until the blessing
comes. The moment of transformation for Jacob is the speaking
of a new name. Jacob becomes Israel, "For as a prince thou hast
power with God and with men and hast prevailed" (Gen. 32:28).
When Jacob finally dares to ask the ultimate question, "Tell me,
I pray thee, thy names" (Gen. 32:29), the blessing is fully given.
The hidden name cannot be humanly spoken, but, as in other
myths, the issue hangs on the asking of the right question at the
right time, though the answer may not be given. Jacob now
knows that in this long struggle of love he has "seen God face to
face" and his life is preserved. It should not be inferred from this
that the "stranger" was God himself, but rather that the new
blessing revealed for a moment the face of God.

Jacob does not come from the struggle unscathed, for the
stranger has touched him in the hollow of his thigh, and he will
be lame from this time forth. We are human and must so remain.
If we dare to wrestle as Jacob did, we may be in some way crip-
pled in ordinary collective living. Without this we would not be
able to stand it. We would rise out of the weakness of our humanity into the *hubris* of fancied equality with the gods. After a
new insight there are two dangers; either an inflation of the ego
may posesses us, or we may fall into discouragement, imagining
that the insight means that we *ought* now to be free of all our old
inadequacies. The "lameness," accepted, cures both these delu-
sions. Indeed we may feel even more inadequate than before on
certain levels.

Jacob is now ready to meet his human brother. No more is said
of his fear. He sends gifts ahead as proof of his friendliness, and
when he meets Esau he finds no rancor in him—indeed, Esau is
almost embarrassingly affectionate. There is an indication in the
text of how deeply Jacob's struggle at the brook was connected
with his brother, inner and outer, when he repeats at the meeting with Esau almost the exact words he had used after the
stranger blessed him. "I have seen thy face," he says to Esau, "as

though I had seen the face of God" (Gen. 33:10). He has not confused the levels of experience—this is evident in the words "as though"—but it seems that his vision of the night before has made possible this seeing of the divine behind the face of his opposite, the long-estranged red brother.

The next pitfall into which Jacob could have fallen now opens before him. Esau, the simple, exuberant fellow, is sure that, all quarrels forgotten, they can settle down to live side by side and have a fine time together! But Jacob's discrimination does not fail. He replies vaguely that he will come later (still wary of crossing his impulsive brother too abruptly) and each goes his separate way in peace. This pitfall is very familiar when we have fought through to freedom from an unconscious dependence or entanglement. We are all too ready to think that now it will be easy to enter into close contact with the people onto whom we used to project our problems. This is usually possible only when the other person involved has also grown toward consciousness to some degree. When a person gives him or herself to the search for individuation, those who are close to that person will either catch the spark, welcome it, and begin to change too, or they will feel threatened by the new freedom and will attack it, consciously or unconsciously. This is an inevitable risk. Except where there is plain human obligation, physical separation is the wiser thing, even for the one who feels himself deserted. Esau would have suffered just as much from Jacob's proximity as vice versa.

Jacob has now a new name; he is a prince inwardly, and in the world wealth and honor lie ahead of him, but nevertheless the new blessing bestowed on him at the brook is the prelude to far greater suffering than any he has yet endured. We persist in imagining that blessing means prosperity. How often we hear people exclaim that they have been greatly blessed, meaning that they have been healthy, happy, with plenty of money in the bank, and how rare it is to hear the recognition of blessing after a catastrophe! Outer events, one way or the other, have little to say about it, but those who carry the blessing will inevitably meet great suffering inwardly.

Jacob now has to suffer in the place where it most hurts, in his sensitive, feeling nature. He was his mother's specially loved son, and the mainspring of his life lay in his intense personal loves. These one by one he must lose.

Rachel is pregnant again, but although Jacob must have known she was delicate and should not travel, he has been told by the voice of God that he must now return to Bethel and build the altar he had promised long ago, and he does not hesitate in his obedience. On the return road, near Bethlehem, Rachel's labor comes upon her, and giving birth to Benjamin, the last and twelfth of his sons, she dies.

All Jacob's love now centers on Rachel's son Joseph, whom he singles out and favors until the jealousy of all the brothers is aroused. Joseph, alone of his sons, Jacob knows, has inherited the inner ear, the capacity to accept the blessing. "Behold this dreamer cometh" (Gen. 37:19), say the contemptuous brothers, and they sell him into Egypt. Now Jacob is alone. The years pass, and the old man's grief for Joseph is still alive in his heart when the brothers bring the extraordinary news of his survival in Egypt. Human feelings do not sublimate themselves with the breakthrough to deeper consciousness. Indeed, the capacity for personal love is thereby increased, and with it the capacity for suffering. Detachment does not mean freedom from love and suffering on the personal level—it means the full opening of the heart to their power and the experience of them, not as an insignificant personal emotion, but as a part of the whole meaning of creation. Detachment is the cessation of personal demand, not the deadening of feeling.

So Jacob journeys to Egypt and is reunited with his son. The time of his death is near, his sons are gathered round his bed, and we read that beautiful chapter in which he sums up the characteristics of each son, each future tribe of Israel. It is sheer poetry, and, most fittingly, the story ends, as it begins, with a blessing. We will quote first the blessing of Jacob himself, as it was understood by Isaac with his limited consciousness. "God give thee of the dew of heaven and the fatness of the earth, and plenty of corn and wine; let people serve thee and nations bow down to thee; be lord over thy brethren, and let thy mother's sons bow down to thee; cursed be everyone that curseth thee, and blessed be he that blesseth thee" (Gen. 28:28–29). Finally, here are the profound and lovely words of Jacob's blessing of Joseph, which seem to sum up the distilled wisdom of his whole life, the blessing, we could say, which may fall on everyone who is willing to be "separate," to stand alone before God.

> . . . the Almighty who shall bless thee with blessings of heaven above, blessings of the deep that lieth under, blessings of the breasts and of the womb; the blessings of thy father have prevailed . . . unto the utmost bound of the everlasting hills; they shall be on the head of Joseph, and on the crown of the head of him that was separate from his brethren (Gen. 49:25–26).

King Lear, by Shakespeare

CORDELIA: For thee, oppressed king, I am cast down;
   Myself could else out-face Fortune's frown.
   Shall we not see these daughters and these sisters?
LEAR: No, no, no, no! Come, let's away to prison:
   We two alone will sing like birds i' th' cage;
   When thou dost ask me blessing, I'll kneel down
   And ask of thee forgiveness. So we'll live,
   And pray, and sing, and tell old tales, and laugh
   At gilded butterflies, and hear poor rogues
   Talk of court news; and we'll talk with them too—
   Who loses and who wins; who's in, who's out—
   And take upon's the mystery of things
   As if we were God's spies; and we'll wear out,
   In a wall'd prison, packs and sects of great ones,
   That ebb and flow by th' moon.

                                   (*Lear* V.iii.5–19)

Surely in all the poetry of the world there could be no more profoundly beautiful, wise, and tender expression of the essence of old age, of the kind of life to which one may come in the last years if one has, like Lear, lived through and accepted all the passion and suffering, the darkness and light, the beauty and horror of one's experience of the world and of oneself.

At a first reading it is easy to miss the profundity, absorbed as we are in the drama, and see it only as a beautiful fantasy of the old man seeking peace behind actual prison walls with his beloved daughter. But on a second, third, and fourth reading, who could fail to realize the immensity of the images, and to see how little an actual dungeon has to do with the story?

Cordelia wishes to go out to meet the evil thing and confront it. Because she is young, this response is true and right. For the old, this is no longer the way—"No, no, no, no! Come, let's away to prison." As a man grows old, his body weakens, his powers fail, his sight perhaps is dimmed, his hearing fades, or his power to move around is taken from him. In one way or another he is "imprisoned," and the moment of choice will come to him. Will he fight this confining process or will he go to meet it in the spirit of King Lear—embrace it with love, with eagerness even? The wisdom of common speech, which we so often miss, speaks to us in the phrase, "He is growing old." We use it indiscriminately about those who are in truth *growing* into old age, into the final flowering and meaning of their lives, and about those who are being dragged into it, protesting, resisting, crying out against their inevitable imprisonment. Only to one who can say with his or her whole being, "Come, let's away to prison," does this chapter apply.

"We two alone will sing like birds i' the cage." We may think of Cordelia in this context as the old man's inner child—the love and courage, the simplicity and innocence of his soul, to which suffering has united him. Cordelia, as Professor Goddard has so beautifully pointed out, while remaining an entirely human person, is also a spirit. Throughout the play she is a symbol of the innocence, the true feeling, that the king so brutally rejected, to which he so blessedly returns, and which, in the instant before death, brings to him, in a flash of vision, the full realization of immortality. So, as the bird pours out notes of joy in its cage, the old man will sing out of his pure love of life in the prison of his enforced inactivity.

Now come those two wonderful lines, "When thou dost ask

me blessing, I'll kneel down and ask of thee forgiveness." If an old person does not feel his need to be forgiven by the young, he or she certainly has not *grown* into age, but merely fallen into it, and his or her "blessing" would be worth nothing. The lines convey with the utmost brevity and power the truth that the blessing that the old may pass on to the young springs only out of that humility that is the fruit of wholeness, the humility that knows *how* to kneel, *how* to ask forgiveness. The old man kneels, not in order to ease guilt feelings (which is at the root of so much apologizing), but in the full and free acceptance of that which Charles Williams so beautifully called *coinherence*. King Lear does not say, "I am not worthy to bless you, only to grovel at your feet." He says, "When you ask me blessing, I'll kneel. . . ." The kneeling *is* the blessing.

"So we'll live," he continues. The exchange of blessing between one human being and another is the essence of life itself. "And pray, and sing, and tell old tales, and laugh at gilded butterflies. . . . " Here are the proper occupations of old age: prayer, which is the quickening of the mind, the rooting of the attention in the ground of being; song, which is the expression of spontaneous joy in the harmony beyond the chaos; the "telling of old tales," which among all primitives was the supreme function of the old, who passed on the wisdom of the ancestors through the symbol, through the understanding of the dreams of the race that their long experience had taught them. In our days how sadly lost, despised even, is this function of the old! Wisdom being identified with knowledge, the "old tale" has become the subject of learned historical research, and only for the few does it remain the carrier of the true wisdom of heart and mind, of body and spirit. When the old cease to "dream dreams," to be "tellers of old tales," the time must come of which the Book of Proverbs speaks: "Where there is no vision the people perish."

And laughter! Surely laughter of a certain kind springs from the heart of those who have truly grown old. It is the laughter of pure delight in beauty—beauty of which the golden butterfly is the perfect symbol—a fleeting, ephemeral thing, passing on the wind, eternally reborn from the earthbound worm, the fragile yet omnipotent beauty of the present moment.

All these four things are activities *without purpose;* any one of them is immediately killed by any hint of striving for achievement. They come to birth only in a heart freed from preoccupation with the goals of the ego, however "spiritual" or lofty these goals may be.

This, however, does not mean that in old age we are to separate ourselves from concern with the world. Without a pause, without even a new sentence, Shakespeare adds to praying, singing, the telling of tales, and laughter an image of listening— listening to the smallest concerns of those still caught in the goals of power. This kind of imprisonment is never a shutting out, a rejection. "And hear poor rogues talk of court news, and we'll talk with them too. Who loses and who wins; who's in, who's out." Not only does the wise old man listen, he responds: "And we'll talk with them too." It is not a matter of listening in a superior manner to problems that the king has outgrown. We feel the smiling tenderness of that phrase "poor rogues," untainted by contempt or boredom, and we can almost hear the old king gravely answering each with his own truth, always interested and concerned, never preaching, but offering to each some glimpse of inner freedom.

There follow the few words that are the climax of the whole speech—only a line and a half—words so moving, of such shining beauty, that if they are heard in the depths of one's being, they can surely never be forgotten but will sing in one's heart for the rest of time. "And take upon's the mystery of things, as if we were God's spies." This is the final responsibility of each person's life. Will we or will we not, as we approach the prison of old age, accept this supreme task? It is not the function of the old to explain or to analyze or to impart information. To them comes the great opportunity of taking upon themselves the mystery of things, of becoming, as it were, God's spies. A spy is one who penetrates into a hidden mystery, and a spy of God is that one who sees at the heart of every manifestation of life, even behind the trivial talk of "poor rogues," the *mysterium tremendum* that is God. Explanations and information, necessary as they are along the way, make clear only partial truths, and the danger of mistaking half-truths for truth itself cannot be exaggerated. We are inclined to use the word "mystery" when we are really speaking of a confused muddle or an ignorant superstition. On the contrary, the true mystery is the eternal paradox at the root of life itself—it is that which, instead of hiding truth, reveals it—the whole, not the part. So, when, after having made every effort to understand, we are ready to take upon ourselves the mystery of things, then the most trivial of happenings is touched by wonder, and there may come to us, by grace, a moment of unclouded vision.

"And we'll wear out in a wall'd prison packs and sects of great ones, that ebb and flow by the moon." "In a wall'd prison" the spirit of the king is free, while those who think they have made themselves great through the instinctive greed of the pack, through fanatical assertion of the rights of sects or party, are the truly imprisoned. They are the ones at the mercy of the ebb and flow of the unconscious forces they despise. The king himself had been one of these "great ones," driven by his lust for flattery, blind to all individual feeling values, dominated by the ebb and flow of the moon, the unconscious, undifferentiated feminine within. But now, at the end, the storm of his suffering has transmuted the lust and cruelty of the pack, of the mob, into tenderness and compassion, has swept away the blind sectarian judgments of his vanity, leaving him alone, a free individual with his Cordelia, his innocence reborn.

"We'll wear out the packs and sects. . . ." What a cry of hope—more than that—of certainty for the human spirit in this world of totalitarian values! One man alone, embracing his prison, reborn into innocence, can "outwear" their terrifying power, not only through patience and suffering, but through prayer and song and laughter and telling of old tales. The rocket and the bomb can never at the last prevail over the golden butterfly. This was Shakespeare's ultimate certainty. "How with this rage shall beauty hold a plea, whose action is no stronger than a flower?" he asks (Sonnet 65). How indeed? And yet it does, he answers in his greatest plays, notably in the miraculous ending of *King Lear*.

Into these twelve brief lines, spoken by an old man of eighty, Shakespeare has condensed all the essential wisdom into which we may hope to grow in our closing years, but they do not speak only to the very old. At every age, to every person, there comes a partial imprisonment, a disabling psychic wound, an unavoidable combination of circumstances, a weakness that we cannot banish, but must simply accept. Necessity in all its forms imprisons us, and, if we could always with a single heart say to our own "Cordelias," "Come, let's away to prison; We two alone will sing like birds i' th' cage," the confining walls would become the alchemist's retort. Inside this retort we would "take upon's the mystery of things," and so the base metal would be transmuted into gold.

How clumsy at the last seem all these words—indeed all words that purport to explain or illuminate great poetry! Yet often we need them to awaken our dulled perception; we speak and hear them in order that we may turn from them again and let the poetry itself speak to us out of silence.

> No, no, no, no! Come, let's away to prison;
> We two alone will sing like birds i' th' cage;
> When thou dost ask me blessing, I'll kneel down
> And ask of thee forgiveness. So we'll live,
> And pray, and sing, and tell old tales, and laugh
> At gilded butterflies, and hear poor rogues
> Talk of court news; and we'll talk with them too—
> Who loses and who wins; who's in, who's out—
> And take upon's the mystery of things
> As if we were God's spies; and we'll wear out,
> In a wall'd prison, packs and sects of great ones,
> That ebb and flow by th' moon.
>
> (*Lear* V.iii.6–19)